GLOBAL POLITICAL FALLOUT

PROGRAM ON INFORMATION RESOURCES POLICY

Harvard University   Center for Information Policy Research

GLOBAL POLITICAL FALLOUT

*The First Decade
of the VCR 1976–1985*

Gladys D. Ganley
Oswald H. Ganley

PROGRAM ON INFORMATION RESOURCES POLICY

Harvard University

*Center for Information
Policy Research*

Cambridge, Massachusetts

Printed in the United States of America.

Library of Congress Cataloging-in-Publication Data

Ganley, Gladys D.
  Global political fallout : the VCR's first decade, 1976–1985 /
Gladys D. Ganley and Oswald H. Ganley.
      p.   cm. — (Communication and information science)
  "A publication of the Porgram on Information Resources Policy"-
-T.p. verso.
  Bibliography: p.
  Includes index.
  ISBN 0-89391-435-5
  1. Video recordings—Political aspects.   2. Video tape recorders
and recording—Political aspects.   I. Ganley, Oswald Harold, 1929-
. II. Harvard University. Program on Information Resources Policy.
III.   Title.   IV. Series.
PN1992.945.G36 1987   87-15155
302.2'34—dc 19   CIP

Ablex Publishing Corporation
355 Chestnut Street
Norwood, New Jersey 07648

PN
1992.945
. G 36

Table of Contents

List of Figures

Acknowledgments

Special thanks are due to the following persons who reviewed and commented critically on drafts of this report. These reviewers and the Program's affiliates are not, however, responsible for or necessarily in agreement with the views expressed herein, nor should they be blamed for any errors of fact or interpretation.

Richard Bissel
Wilson Dizard
Kenton W. Elderkin
Roy Godson
Robert A. Martin
David C. McGaffey
David Y. McManis
Yunosuke Ohkura
Charles Oliver
Alan H. Protheroe
Rosemary Righter
Hewson Ryan
William Salmon
Michael D. Schneider
W. Scott Thompson
Nils H. Wessell
Julia B. Wetzel
Raymond Vernon

Our very special thanks go to those people who contributed to our efforts by the personal communications seen in Appendix A and included throughout the paper. Their information not only enriched the study greatly, but has also served as a "quality control" tool and guide to other research sources. We would like to express our deep appreciation.

Executive Summary

It is now, as of the mid-1980s, one decade since videocassette recorders (VCRs) and videocassettes became generally available to private users. This is the second electronic medium—the first was the audiocassette and recorder—to permit creative control by individuals over program selection and information content.

In these 10 years, VCRs and at least representative specimens of the entire spectrum of programming available in democracies have penetrated into even the most restrictive nations, often in large quantities. Their distribution has been greatly aided by widespread black markets, ample smuggling routes, organized crime groups, cassette pirates, large numbers of migrant workers, and a variety of (often hidden) discretionary incomes in theoretically poor countries. This is occurring despite hundreds of years of government censorship of other media in most nations. Despite widespread bans on both VCRs and videocassette programming, people globally are at present viewing almost whatever they choose to. Videocassettes have also been used to perpetrate specific political acts, such as spreading propaganda, supporting rebel guerrilla activities, airing the views of and assisting terrorists, sending messages across borders where individuals are unwelcome, avoiding governmental news blackouts, passing off lobbying as news, and spreading anti-Semitism. They have been used for political purposes by governments as well as by individuals.

The means of control thus far instituted by even the most restrictive governments do not appear to be commensurate with the threat posed by VCRs and videocassettes to the information monopolies claimed by many nations. Where controls have been rather rigorously attempted, they have usually been ineffective. This is true even in those countries where information suppression is a high art, such as the USSR and the countries of Eastern Europe. Not even the death sentences imposed by the Islamic government of Iran have stopped the free flow of banned videocassettes on that country's black market. The result is that, at least for the time being, a sort of *de facto* global media decentralization has been effected.

Videocassette uses are following in the footsteps of audiocassettes, which were an integral and essential tool for fomenting and carrying out Ayatollah Khomeini's Iranian Islamic revolution. But videocassettes have the additional impact of a picture, and the ability to more effectively disperse the messages of two powerful media, world films and television.

The use of VCRs and videocassettes is still in its infancy. Indications are that this new medium will have an important, perhaps critical, global political impact of wide range and scope in the perhaps not-too-distant future.

CHAPTER ONE

Introduction

By 1985, more than 60 million videocassette recorders (VCRs)* had been distributed globally in the decade since 1976, when they began to be used to any extent by private individuals. This number was expected to climb to 100 million by 1986, and all indications are that it will go on growing.[1] U.S. companies, which hold about 60% of the world's pre-recorded videocassette market, expected to sell around $1.5 billion worth in 1985, triple the 1982 figure.[2]** The world market in legally sold videocassettes is nearly $2.5 billion annually, and there is an illegal market of pirated and smuggled cassettes that matches or more probably exceeds this figure.

VCRs, blank tapes, pre-recorded videocassette films, and TV programming are all being snapped up by people globally. Both VCRs and cassettes are now simple to use. It is easy for an amateur to record material off the air, to edit or alter it, or to produce videotapes using blank cassettes and a home camera. (Both VCR and camera are often rentable.)

Videocassette programming can presently be easily and rapidly duplicated to share with others. Whatever the programming, it can be watched in privacy, wherever a television set is available. It is not necessary to have a broadcast signal to use a VCR. VCRs and videocassettes therefore often substitute for broadcast television. Since many sources have indicated that video impresses people much more than audio or printed material, this access makes for a possibly volatile political situation.

For several reasons, large numbers of VCRs have always been smuggled: to obtain them cheaper; to avoid taxes, registration, and licensing; and to bring them into countries such as Iran, most major communist countries, and many other nations, where they are prohibited or heavily restricted. Although countries may also wish to keep out VCRs to control information, restrictions are, with some regularity, made initially on an economic basis.

Little programming for VCRs existed when they first became available. Because this medium offered the new opportunity to privately watch pornography, dealers in pirated and smuggled "blue" videocassettes quickly became active. But this underground porno route was almost immediately

---

* The words "videocassette recorder (VCR)" and "videocassette" will ordinarily be used in this study, but they are synonymous with "videotape recorder (VTR)" and "videotape."

** Ninety percent of all VCRs are made in Japan. Blank tapes are made mainly in Europe and the Far East. Americans and Europeans dominate the pre-recorded cassette market, but videocassette programming is being produced in many countries.[3]

found also to be ideal for circumventing long waits for release and other obstacles to programming access (not the least of them copyright ownership). Soon, both illegal and legal cassettes with unlimited sorts of content were flooding across the world's borders. Rental dealerships mushroomed globally, offering programming for a fraction of the cost of movies, along with massive supplies of blank videocassettes.

This global blitz by VCRs and videocassettes is permitting the wholesale circumvention of government censorship of the content of film and television programming. This is no small thing, since, in most of the world, media content, especially that of film, radio, and television, is strictly controlled by governments. From antiquity onward, government control of information has been the rule, not the exception. In modern times, even in democracies, censorship of the mass media has been only slowly and partially lifted. Says the *World Press Review*:

> Each year the International Press Institute publishes its annual World Press Freedom Review and each year the situation continues to grow worse.
>
> The 1983 IPI survey shows that today only a small part of the globe respects free speech. The rest of the world is "gagged" . . . .[4]

For information controls to have endured throughout the centuries and to still be in place, governments must consider that their stakes in maintaining them surpass most concerns. Examples have been surfacing that make it obvious that not all uses of VCRs and videocassettes are politically innocuous. This study was therefore undertaken to determine the political stakes of various world governments in maintaining or regaining rapidly eroding national controls over film and TV programming content. Some questions addressed were:

- What is the potential for VCRs and programming to be used for political subversion or as propaganda tools? How much of this is already happening?
- To what extent are VCRs and videocassettes destabilizing? To what extent are they democratizing?
- Are VCRs and videocassettes different in any significant way from older, often cheaper forms of communications?
- Are governments attempting to stem this VCR and videocassette flow across their borders?
- What controls are being applied, and what is the degree of their effectiveness? If controls are not being effectively applied, then why not? What are other, perhaps higher, government priorities?

Since this is such a new and rapidly evolving medium, and its scope of use is global, press reports have had to be heavily relied on for information. But to focus more sharply on the political aspects of VCR and videocassette spread and uses, and to obtain first-hand information, the authors contacted one or more individuals thought to be knowledgeable about VCR activities in approximately 30 countries and, in one instance, a region. Anonymity was assured, to permit frankness in answering either mail or personal interview queries. It will thus be stated only that all these contacts are Americans, and all either reside in, travel frequently to, or are otherwise thoroughly familiar with the involved country or region. Although they occasionally varied in detail, these personal communications as a whole complemented press statements. Some of the communications have been used in the body of this report, but, because the answers were extensive and because this information is not available elsewhere, excerpts from the compiled communications are included in Appendix A.

This paper first looks briefly at the status of global dissemination of other electronic information technologies, and government controls over them, as VCRs and videocassettes make their appearance. It examines audiocassettes and recorders (the first of these technologies to permit user control and input of content) for their political uses, and finds them to be purveyors of political music, speeches, poetry, plays, and even disinformation. In one case, Iran, they were instrumental in fomenting and carrying out a revolution. This paper explores in depth the penetration of VCRs and videocassettes, especially by means which are unusual or illegal and therefore less controllable. It describes the power of migrant workers to pressure governments to permit VCR entry. It devotes special attention to the contributions of black markets and organized crime to the deep penetration of VCRs and videocassettes into countries where entry might otherwise be forbidden or heavily restricted. It discusses what people choose to watch globally, and a variety of settings for watching VCRs outside the home. Other chapters cover the concerns that governments have expressed about VCRs and videocassettes, and political acts that have been committed via the VCR and videocassette medium. Finally, the paper looks at the measures taken by governments to control VCRs and videocassettes, and the reasons for their general ineffectiveness.

Because the subject is so broad, much has had to be omitted. The issue of copyright ownership — or international intellectual property violations — is not discussed, except in the sense that violations of ownership make possible more rapid and prolific information dissemination. Histories of political uses of older media could not be gone into extensively. The uses of VCRs and videocassettes for educational purposes globally, with their own wide-reaching political dimension, have also been omitted.

A strenuous attempt was made to tie the material to the traditional political blocs of countries — the democracies, the communist world, and the developing nations. But a globalness was found that defied this treatment: Videocassette piracy is totally global in nature; smuggling of VCRs and cassettes is omnipresent; the rich, in democracies, are as willing to cheat on VCR taxes or hide from VCR registration as are the poor in repressive nations; governments decry pornography, yet it is being watched universally; Great Britain has been quicker to seek restrictive videocassette laws than has China or the Soviet Union; migrant couriers of VCRs and cassettes cross all sorts of world borders; black markets globally deal in these much-sought-after new items; illegal machines and tapes are bought worldwide, despite apparent lack of income; and specific political acts using VCRs and cassettes have been discovered to have occurred in a wide variety of settings. A most important global feature is that, although VCRs and cassettes are often unwanted by governments, no government, including that of the USSR, has yet been able to put a stop to them. Douglas Boyd and Joseph Straubhaar have succinctly described the global effects of VCRs and videocassettes on those countries who would, in whatever way, bridle their media. VCRs, they say, "have brought to many countries de facto media decentralization. . . ."[5] This paper contends that this has happened to some extent in most countries.

VCRs and videocassettes represent the fulfilment of some of the world's wildest fantasies. They symbolize the usurpation of control by private individuals over a mass source of information, a control that many governments consider their domain. VCRs and videocassettes offer individuals in lesser developed nations some control over a new technology. They permit easy production and dissemination of materials to wide audiences without the necessity for an official institution. In perhaps the wildest fantasy of all, VCRs and videocassettes symbolize control over Hollywood and other such dream empires. For they are breaking the monopolies on distribution long held by a few film production centers, and are broadening the kinds of global materials available. That the machine making it all possible is not an American, nor for the most part a European, but a Japanese machine, may represent another potent symbol of shift in political power.

By routinely ignoring formal bans on VCRs and videocassette programming, users in restrictive countries are striking at governmental legitimacy. *Radio Free Europe Research* says of the "major storm" of VCRs and videocassette programming now reaching the Soviet bloc countries:

> the proliferation of video recording and playback equipment and of illegally produced and procured programs have been presenting a direct challenge not only to their monopoly of power over the media but also to the strictly regulated legal order of their states. . . .[6]

Upon seeing a videotaped movie for the first time, the elderly uncle of a Soviet journalist may have said it all by exclaiming, " 'What a blow to the
Bolsheviks!' "[7]

The political use of VCRs and videocassettes is still a breaking story, and
there must of necessity be holes and inconsistencies in the presented data.
But the new trails being broken through the forest of governmental and other
controls on global information access are already becoming clearly discernible.

NOTES

[1]"U.S. Cassette Recorder Count at 13,200,000; 57,000,000 Worldwide," *Variety*, October
17, 1984, p. 2.

Richard Klein, "Pic Assn.'s Nix Gives Antipiracy Advice to Members of AFMA," *Variety*,
December 12, 1984, p. 6.

" '85 VCR Count to Tally 100-Mil, Predicts MPEA," *Variety*, February 27, 1985, p. 37.

[2]Tom Bierbaum, "See 1985 Sales of Videocassettes Up to 33,000,000 Units," *Variety*,
January 16, 1985, p. 1.

[3]J. L. Battenfeld, "VHS Snares 80% of Video Market, Sony Losing 'Battle of the Formats',"
The Boston Globe, January 28, 1985, p. 44.

Ken Terry, "Blank Tape Market is Dominated By Foreigners; BASF Tops Chrome,"
Variety, January 30, 1985, p. 77.

[4]"Surveying World Press Freedom. Weighing Gains and Losses of 1983," *World Press Review*,
February 1984, p. 58.

[5]Douglas A. Boyd and Joseph D. Straubhaar, "Developmental Impact of the Home Video
Cassette Recorder on Third World Countries," *Journal of Broadcasting & Electronic Media*,
Volume 29, Number 1, Winter 1985, p. 9.

[6]Steven Koppany, "Unprepared Regime Scrambles to Meet Challenges of the Video Era,"
Situation Report, Hungary/10, *Radio Free Europe Research*, Radio Free Europe-Radio Liberty,
September 4, 1985, p. 17.

[7]Robert Kaiser, "Russian Life: Is 'Veedeyo' A Blow to the Bolsheviks?" *The Washington Post*,
September 9, 1984, p. D-10.

CHAPTER TWO

The Environment for Entry of VCRs and Videocassettes with Special Emphasis on Audio Recorders and Cassettes

VCRs and videocassettes were preceded globally by transistor radios, records, television, global satellite transmission, and audio recorders and cassettes. Radio and television brought extensive amusement and information into many areas worldwide, but, unless signals could be picked up across borders (often from another protected country), programming remained strictly controlled by national governments. Clandestine radio cropped up at times in some countries. Some people received outside broadcasts from Voice of America, Radio Free Europe, Radio Moscow, etc. Records offered individuals the chance to choose the type of information they wanted, but this was largely limited to music. It remained for audio recorders and cassettes to provide any substantial power over the creation of electronic content to compare with writing in the print medium.

Television was deliberately introduced into many countries—Saudi Arabia, for instance—because it was thought to be, and was for a long time, controllable. Boyd says:

> Saudi Arabia, as only one example in the Gulf states, decided to introduce television in the mid-1960s because leaders believed that it would be an ideal medium in this Islamic family-oriented society and that the government would be the cultural, as well as the entertainment and information, gatekeeper. . . .[1]

Saudi Arabia, ironically, became the first and among the most intense of the "videotape societies," a limited number of half-inch, reel-to-reel Sony videotape recorders being brought in as early as 1967.[2]

Television was deliberately *not* introduced into Tanzania, in an attempt to keep out unwanted information. Here, President Julius Nyerere, in power in a one-party system since Tanzania gained independence from Great Britain in 1961, believed that*

> TV . . . [was] a vicious means of exposing the mass public to the influence of world capitalism and imperialism . . . .[3]

---

* There were also, and still are, financial reasons.

Nyerere was, however, defeated in his intent. Despite a 1974 ban on television imports, people smuggled in sets to pick up signals from neighboring Kenya, Uganda, and semi-autonomous off-shore Zanzibar. With the advent of VCRs, and despite an extensive early 1980s crackdown, they then smuggled in VCRs and cassettes and even set up underground shops for video rentals.[4] In 1983, Nyerere capitulated and lifted the various import bans.[5] Although the country still has no broadcasting system, TV is to be had from alternate sources.

Mainly for financial reasons — quality programming can be had very cheaply* — but also because it is tremendously popular, U.S. industries have dominated television programming globally.[6] "Dallas," as just one example of a host of American programs, is seen in 97 countries.[7]** Even the Soviet Union and Eastern Europe watch selected American shows. However, television programming is generally carefully chosen and censored to meet the perceived needs of governments.

National control over television has been eroding to some extent. White South Africans in Johannesburg have been eager to pick up signals from the black "homeland" Bophutha Tswana, dubbed Bop-TV. Aimed at black townships, but "spilling" over into white areas, it sometimes quotes banned South Africans and offers some material by anti-apartheid leaders.[11] The East German government has given up trying to keep its people from picking up West German television, and, in a bid to stem internal migration, is even providing cable to transmit West German programming to remote parts of the country.[12] To regain the interest of its viewers, the GDR has introduced 10 full length films (35% of them from Western nations) into its weekly TV programming. These are so popular that West Germans, especially West Berliners, are joining the Easterners in watching.[13] The Israeli government, which first delayed introducing television, and then delayed color television, to protect its people, has been unable to keep said citizens from tuning in Jordan as a "second channel."[14] Many parts of European nations currently receive the signals of neighboring countries. This includes Eastern European nations such as Czechoslovakia and Hungary, and even to some extent the Soviet Union.[15] In addition, cable TV and the illegal interception of satellite signals are creating further programming freedom, and direct broadcasting by satellite (DBS-TV) is expected to contribute to this freedom in the near future.

---

* As compared to original production. Producers of U.S. programming mainly regain their production costs domestically. The cost to foreigners mostly represents profit, and can therefore be very reasonable.

** Although its share of the world market is said to be declining, the U.S. exports more than $1 billion worth of films and TV programs a year. U.S. videocassette exports (excluding those pirated) are worth $500 million annually.[8] "Little House on the Prairie" is seen in 104 countries, and "The Love Boat" is seen in 85.[9] Bangladesh, for instance, sees "Dallas," "Dynasty," "Charlie's Angels," "MASH," and "Little House on the Prairie."[10]

Aside from censorship for moral, cultural, religious, and political reasons, and just plain poor or inadequate programming, TV is considered
unsatisfactory in many countries because it is used excessively for religious
harangue or government propaganda.* In Togo, said to be representative of
most French-speaking African countries, the president, General Eyadema,
personally dominates most television broadcasts. Both the 8:00 and the
10:00 p.m. news broadcasts feature his speeches, him presiding at ceremo-
nies, and parades in his honor.[16] One Togo announcer delayed a late-
arriving presidential message (a carbon of all presidential messages) from
the 8:00 p.m. until the later broadcast. Post-broadcast, he found soldiers
waiting to take him to the president, who posed the question: " 'Is Togo television yours or mine?' "[17] He then learned whose it was by being docked two
months' salary and ordered off the air indefinitely.

In Iran, television is sometimes called "mullah-vision" or "the woolly
glass," for the endless procession of bearded mullahs it features, or who wan-
der, aimlessly preaching, through scheduled programs.[18] In Pakistan, there
is a joke circulating that people call the TV repairman to have him remove
the mullah trapped in their television.[19]

The result of such government dominance is that, where there is an
alternative, people stop watching television broadcasts. In Kenya, for example, it is said that

> [Kenya VCR] owners now rarely tune in television — where the President can
> be seen nightly on the news — in favor of watching American films.[20]

The other form of visual entertainment, the cinema, has always been
controlled and censored in some way in every country, including democracies. This has been relatively easy to enforce, since showings are largely restricted both by law and by economics to easily visible public places. But
here, too, the audience may defeat the government. In Eastern Europe, for
instance, people just won't go to see films that show only what the regime
wants to show them. *The Wall Street Journal* says that, in Czechoslovakia,

> publishers, movie houses, theaters and record stores still must fulfil their re-
> spective plans; they have to show profits for the comrades in charge to get their
> bonuses. . . .[21]

So they are bringing in popular movies like "E.T." and other Western products to help make up the deficit.

The freedom not only to select content, but to alter it or create it, arrived
globally with the audiotape and tape recorder. A political use of audiotape

---

* In the U.S., this includes excessive advertising.

was made as early as World War II, "when speeches by Hitler and other prominent Nazi leaders were broadcast at times and places calculated to confuse Allied intelligence . . . ."[22] The audiocassette recorder became generally available to individuals in the early 1960s. In a number of countries, its creative capability has found political uses.[23]

The most systematic and successful use of audiocassettes for political purposes has been that of Ayatollah Khomeini, for whom they were an integral and essential part of a successful revolution. From 1965, when he took up residence in exile in Najaf, Iraq, through his Paris stay from October 1978 to the end of January 1979, both smuggled audiocassettes (often brought into Iran by Iranian pilgrims to Iraq) and the recorded copies of Khomeini's direct-dialed telephone conversations to Iran were consistently used by his followers. First, they were employed to build up support for an Islamic takeover of the government, and then, as the revolution gained steam, for Khomeini to direct, step-by-step from exile, the unseating of the regime of Shah Mohammed Reza Pahlavi.[24]* Khomeini has now moved on to use both audio and videocassettes to propagate his message internally.[26] He is also said to use audiocassettes and videocassettes for political propaganda externally, with Egypt and Turkey mentioned as targets.[27] Following the Soviet intervention in Afghanistan, audiocassettes of Khomeini's speeches are said to have begun circulating in the black markets of Soviet Central Asia.[28]

In another volatile country, India, audiocassettes have also found political uses. *The New York Times* reported in May 1985 that cassettes of speeches of the late radical Sikh leader, Jarmail Singh Bhindrawale, "are widely circulated throughout the Punjab . . . ."[29] One can speculate that they were used to spread his messages while he was living. Bhindrawale was killed during the invasion by the Indian military of the Sikh's Golden Temple in Amritsar in early June 1984. This invasion probably led to the assassination of Prime Minister Indira Ghandi the following November.

The *World Press Review* reports that, in the Middle East, an audiocassette "culture" evolved in the mid-1970s. It spread out from Egypt and Lebanon, and has produced many production centers and "a variety of 'stars' of the underground culture." According to this article:

> the Arab cassette culture addresses every aspect of art and society: underground poetry, popular poetry, religion, politics, economics, philosophy, songs in all Arabic dialects as well as classical Arabic, and off-the-record news and political analysis.[30]

---

* So much is heard about Khomeini's ingenious uses of various information technologies in promulgating his revolution — including his use of direct long-distance telephone dialing — that it is amusing to learn the Iraqis, who gave him political refuge from 1963 to 1978, say he left their country without paying his telephone bill.[25]

Among famous cassette culture stars is the blind Egyptian lutist, Sheikh Imam, who has been repeatedly imprisoned by Presidents Sadat and Mubarak.[31] Possession of Sheikh Imam's tapes will bring up to 10 years in jail in Jordan, Saudi Arabia, Oman, and Bahrain.[32] His underground music is said to be more popular than that of Egyptian artists who broadcast freely over 102 Arab stations.[33] Sheikh Imam and many other singers can be heard on the several radio stations run by Maghreb and Middle Eastern immigrant communities in Paris, which sometimes broadcast " 'things which are not said in our own countries. . . .' "[34]

Marcel Khalifa, a Lebanese Maronite, circulates contemporary poetry via audiotape among Arab youth. His songs stress, among other things, the need for social change, for unity of the region, and for new opportunities for Arab women.[35] Khalifa came to the U.S. in 1982 to give sold-out concerts. His fame, like that of other underground audiotape stars, was so great that,

> during his concerts the audience packed the theaters, singing his songs along with him although the music had never been broadcast.[36]

Middle Eastern plays, many of which are politically oriented, are widely broadcast on television and circulated on audiocassettes.[37]* Tape recorders are very popular with the poor of Cairo. Nine families who, in 1969 had eight radios and three black and white TVs among them, in 1982 owned nine radios, nine TVs (six of them color), and six tape recorders.[38]

In Malaysia, audiotaped messages by political leaders were used in a 1984 conflict between members of the ruling Muslim party, UMNO, and the fundamentalist Muslim minority party, PAS. The issue being debated centered around who was and who was not "a true believer." (See Chapter 8). Ceremahs, or political-religious lectures by fiery PAS orators, were circulated on audiocassettes, and led to a massive "counter-cassette" effort by the leaders of UMNO. UMNO newspapers were reported as saying:

> each of UMNO's 7,615 branches is under orders to identify powerful orators among its members to redress the opposition's perceived rhetorical advantage. The effective circulation of tape-recorded ceremahs by such orators as Pas vice-president Ustaz Hadi Awang will be met by "counter-cassettes". . . .[39]

In July 1984, Home Affairs Minister Radzi Ahmad told the Malaysian parliament that the government intended to "clamp down on" religious cassette circulation.[40] The *Index on Censorship* interpreted this to mean that the Malaysian government's political opposition would be curbed.[41] But, as the first use of a new Printing Presses and Publications Act in January 1985, the

---

* As well as on videocassettes, which are now very popular.

Minister instead banned three Indonesian audiocassettes containing political messages for its own country.[42]

In Poland, audiotapes are part of a greatly stepped-up post-Solidarity underground or "independent" culture which supplements lectures by leading figures through churches, the clandestine performances of political cabarets in apartments, "flying universities," and other covert actions.[43] Political lectures or songs on audiocassettes are said to be widely duplicated and distributed.[44] Effective control by the Polish government of clandestine broadcasting, especially, has led to an emphasis on underground audiocassette production and distribution. *Poland Watch* reports that

> these include cassettes with anti-government songs recorded in underground cabarets, internment camps, and prisons; recordings of historical events from the time when Solidarity existed legally; and interviews with leaders of the Underground. The most recent phenomenon is the so-called "Bratkowski's Gazette." The President of the banned Polish Journalists' Association, Stefan Bratkowski, records on tape his comments and remarks on current events and reads texts he considers worth disseminating. . . . [45]

The "Gazette" is receiving quite wide distribution. When the Pope visited Poland, his sermons were recorded from the Vatican Radio — for which Radio Free Europe got a feed — and widely distributed, because Polish broadcasts were thought to be too "selective." During the height of Solidarity, that group's use of blank audiocassettes was so extensive that it caused a shortage to develop in Poland. The government then simply did not make new supplies available, because they were being used for political purposes.[46] Audiocassette recorders and audiocassettes are said to be ordinarily freely available in Poland.

Audiocassettes were being used to a certain extent during the formation of Solidarity. Timothy Ash describes the scene inside the Health and Safety hall of the Lenin Shipyard in Gdansk in the early days of the August 1980 strike which launched the movement. Here, delegates to the Interfactory Strike Committee (the MKS) met at three tables the length of the assembly hall, "beneath the Polish flag and the cross," with the base of Lenin's statue being used as a "convenient shelf for empty tea mugs."

> At the back of the hall . . . [was] a bank of electronic equipment: the amplifiers and relays which had supplanted the works radio, and a small forest of private cassette-recorders. These products of the Gierek boom played an important role in the organization. Almost every day the delegates returned to their workplaces . . . to report to their mates with a cassette-recording of the day's high spots. In many factories this recording was actually broadcast over the works radio. In the Lenin, I noticed a small group amusing themselves by lis-

tening to a tape of Gierek's meeting with the shipyard workers in this very hall in 1971. They would not be fooled so easily this time around![47]

In the occupied West Bank, " 'hundreds of cassettes with nationalistic songs' "[48] were confiscated by Israeli military authorities in March 1985, along with books on bomb building and guerilla warfare, anti-Israeli posters, and flags of the Palestine Liberation Organization.[49] These were said to have been planned for use in an exhibit by students at the Palestinian-run Bir Zeit University to celebrate the PLO's 16th anniversary. Israeli law defines this group as a terrorist organization. About 50 people were arrested, and the University temporarily closed. There have been closings for similar reasons of Bethlehem University.[50]

In Ecuador in summer 1985, armed members of the revolutionary group Alfaro Vive took over a radio station in Quito. "They tied up the staff and played revolutionary and anti-government tapes before escaping."[51]

An interesting possible use of audiocassettes is by dissidents in the Seychelles Islands. This island group, 1000 miles off the coast of Africa in the Indian Ocean, is regarded as one of the many potential "Little Grenadas." The Islands

> lie on the supertanker route between the Cape of Good Hope and the Persian Gulf, and they can electronically keep an eye on the important U.S. naval base 600 mi. away on the tiny island of Diego Garcia.[52]

The base is described as "a crucial jump-off point for U.S. naval and air power protecting the Persian Gulf oil-supply routes and U.S. ships in the Indian Ocean. . . ."[53] Soviet surrogates from East Germany, Cuba, North Korea, and Libya support Albert F. Rene and his "hardline communist sympathizers. . . ." This group took over in 1977, and there has been at least one attempted coup, in 1981, against it.*

The Seychelles situation is described by one writer[55] as a microcosm of a worldwide post-World War II problem, where tiny countries have become independent but were thought to have been rendered powerless by being bypassed by modern communications.** Instead, they are becoming hot-

---

* In mid-1985, the last cinema in the Seychelles closed its doors, victim of the video rental shops "which flooded the market with the latest . . . [box office] hits. . . ."[54]

** Some other "Little Grenadas" are Surinam (formerly Dutch Guiana) at "Brazil's back door," which is undergoing a Cuban arms buildup; former French and British possessions in the South Pacific (such as New Caledonia, whose independence agitators are accused of being pro-Russian), and the former Portuguese colony of Guinea-Bissau, on the West Coast of Africa.[46] The Kanuks, native advocates of New Caledonian independence, are said to have sought training for some of their people in Libya. The *Far Eastern Economic Review* says that critics of independence, "stress New Caledonia's crucial geopolitical significance in the face of the Soviet Unbeds of political activity, just when new communications technologies are offering them new opportunities.

That audiocassettes are popular in the Soviet Union underground was affirmed when the visit of the Reverend Billy Graham to Russia prompted the comment:

> The evangelist's words are likely to be heard by more than those who came to see him; surreptitious cassette recorders will doubtless give his sermons wide distribution among Soviets. . . .[58]

As is true in Poland, audio recorders and cassettes are quite readily available in the Soviet Union. The USSR, says Donald Shanor of Columbia University, produced about half a million tape recorders in 1965, but upped this to a million in 1970, to 2 million in 1975, and to 3 million annually in the 1980s.[59]* Used mainly, he admits, for harmless family recordings, entertainment, and communications, these recorders are also used to store and relay underground oral literature, protest songs and poems, and to "capture and preserve some of the programs carried by the foreign broadcasts."[61] Shanor says

> tape recorders go along on picnics, not only to play the songs that are never broadcast on Soviet stations, but to be coupled with shortwave radios. They record foreign broadcasts of news, commentary, and more forbidden music, with the signals clear because the picnic site is out of reach of the city jammers . . . .[62]

Radio Liberty's 700 hours of broadcasts of the full *The Gulag Archipelago*, he says, are on tape in "many collections" in the USSR, and tapes of outside news of the downing of Korean Airline Flight 007 are among the many circulating "classics."[63]

Soviet-produced shortwave radios, which by 1975 numbered 60 million, are made "without the high frequency bands used by foreign broadcasters . . . ."[64] But, according to Shanor, the necessary parts for conversion can be bought at Soviet electrical hobby shops, and rewiring is quite simple. For about $1500, a Western or Japanese model radio-tape recorder can be had.

---

ion's expanding military presence in the region. The Soviet presence in the South Pacific to date is limited. But not long after its recent independence, neighboring Vanuatu established diplomatic relations with Cuba and there is fear in Paris it may be prepared to offer port facilities to the Soviet Pacific fleet."[57]

* By comparison, *The New York Times* reports that, in summer 1985, "85% of American households have at least one cassette player, 60% have car players and 50% have portable players." It quotes one source as saying that " 'There are now more cassette players in American households than television sets.' "[60]

Some of these in the Ukraine are brought in by Soviet sailors.[65] Rewiring of the radios also goes on elsewhere. In Poland, for instance, slight tinkering with an American FM radio makes it capable of picking up the Polish police band.[66] This permitted listening in by individuals during Solidarity demonstrations. Strikers at the Lenin shipyard in Gdansk in August 1980, <u>Reuters</u> says,

> got some light relief . . . by listening to monitored conversations from police vans beamed over a public address system. The conversations between two patrol vans were tapped by a sympathetic radio-taxi driver who could tune into the police frequency. There was laughter from the strikers as they heard: "Green Fiat coming from Wrzeszcz throwing out leaflets. Follow him."[67]

Smuggled audiocassettes with religious content are also said to be a special problem to authorities in Soviet-held Estonia.[68]

The Soviet government has used audiocassettes to distribute disinformation. In early 1984, for instance, *UPI* reported circulation of "tapes of fake conversations between President Reagan and other world leaders" thought to have originated with the KGB. The tapes of Reagan, Margaret Thatcher, and others had been "spliced together from public speeches," and while "the voices are authentic . . . the words spoken have been doctored, cut, rearranged on tape and then worked into the transcript. . . ."[69] One tape, appearing in Holland, had Reagan saying, "If there is a conflict we shall fire missiles at our allies to see to it that the Soviet Union stays within its borders. . . ."[70] and Margaret Thatcher, through heavy static, as if via telephone, saying " 'You mean Germany?' " Reagan's "reply" was " 'Mrs. Thatcher, if any country endangers our position we can decide to bomb the problem area and so remove the instability.' "[71] Other tapes had astronaut Neil Armstrong converting to Islam after his moon landing, and Defense Secretary Weinberger " 'offering Saudi Arabia tanks that are "not even in the hands of the American army". . . .' "[72]

On the first day of Ayatollah Khomeini's government in Iran, a disinformation audiocassette was circulated. That is:

> the Islamic movement made public a tape recording, allegedly of the Shah briefing his ranking commanders and calling for the armed forces to instigate prolonged civil war. Though it was analyzed later as a forgery by voice experts in the United States and Britain . . . it [was used] effectively . . . to discredit the military, particularly its senior leadership.[73]

Big portable audiocassette radios and even bigger non-portables are all the rage in China.[74] Individuals newly "rich" through China's "responsibility system," introduced to encourage private initiative, are very eager to buy them. They can be had at foreign currency Friendship Stores run by the Chinese government. Theoretically, Chinese individuals are not allowed to make purchases in these stores, which are reserved for foreigners and overseas Chinese with hard currency. Resident Chinese are not supposed to have hard currency, either, but they get it one way or another. Such niceties as identity are overlooked by the Friendship Store clerks " 'If you dress up like an overseas Chinese. . .' "[75] because, if they make a sale, they get a bonus.

In China, smuggled audiocassettes from Hong Kong and elsewhere are so popular that the government, as a prelude to the short-lived 1983 crackdown on "spiritual pollution," compiled a guidebook entitled *How to Distinguish Decadent Songs.*[76] The authorities were said to be at least as upset by sentimental ballads from Taiwan and Hong Kong as by Western music.[77] In a report on intellectual freedom in China in the 1980s, Liang Heng and Judith Shapiro say that, before and during the spiritual pollution campaign, the main target of the Chinese was light music. With the opening of the door to the West, light music had entered from Hong Kong and Taiwan. People had also become able to buy large tape recorders, which they used to hold dances and to take to parks "to impress their friends." The Taiwanese singer Deng Lijun was especially popular. But these light lyrics,

> often sentimental and individualistic, were seen as "bourgeois drugs," weakening the young people's revolutionary energy. The singing styles, soft and sexy, were seen as dangerous pollution. However, the well-distributed bootleg tapes, both smuggled in and illegally manufactured within China, were clearly not going to be eradicated overnight. As the joke said, China was "governed by the two Dengs: during the day people listened to Deng Xiaoping, at night, to Deng Lijun."[78]

Anthropologist Steven Mosher, who wrote a book about his 1979–1980 stay in a Chinese village, makes many mentions of the uses of audiocassettes and recorders.[79] The recorders were even at that time a favorite item demanded as bribes by local governing cadres. These bribes were necessary to get them to distribute other "treasures" (consumer goods), allocate jobs, permit businesses, or allow "rusticated" urban youth to return to the city.[80] Tape recorders were included, along with TV sets, wrist watches, and hand calculators, among the coveted Four Modernizations.[81] And, among the 10 attributes of an ideal Chinese husband (along with dead parents, estranged relatives, and "first rate talent") he should own "a bike, a sewing machine, a tape recorder, and a television. . . ."[82]

In Vietnam, says the *Index on Censorship,* an army newspaper wrote in October 1985 that

> "reactionary and decadent" music was particularly marked in Ho Chi Minh City and the enemy was using Western pop music to "attack us by poisoning

the public with reactionary and decadent cassettes." The paper urged people to listen to Vietnamese music which is "pure and healthy" and "encourages people to surmount difficulties. . . ."[83]

Audio recorders and cassettes have thus penetrated globally, even into usually protected environments and across various levels of society. They have been employed for political purposes on numerous occasions, and have even been instrumental in the successful staging of a revolution. But audio lacks the impact of a picture, and is incapable of effectively transmitting the messages of the two extremely powerful mass media, film and television, or the drama of the theater. This has been left to videocassettes and the videocassette recorder.

NOTES

[1]Douglas A Boyd and Joseph D. Straubhaar, "Developmental Impact of the Home Video Cassette Recorder on Third World Countries," *Journal of Broadcasting & Electronic Media*, Volume 29, Number 1, Winter 1985, p. 11.

[2]*Ibid.*, p. 10.

[3]Ludovick A. Ngatara, "Economy Down, Video Up," *InterMedia*, July/September, 1983, p. 71.

[4]*Ibid.*, and also:

"Dateline: Dar Es Salaam, Tanzania," *United Press International*, November 5, 1982 (NEXIS).

Nguyen Anh Tuyet, "Moslem Asian Countries Flex Political Muscles," *United Press International*, November 15, 1982 (NEXIS).

Glenn Frankel, "Tanzanian President Planning to Retire After 23 Years as Third World Leader," *The Boston Globe*, December 12, 1984, p. A-26.

"Nyerere Strolls on Towards Never-never Land," *The Economist*, October 20, 1984, p. 33.

[5]Ludovick A. Ngatara, "Economy Down, Video Up," *InterMedia*, July/September, 1983, p. 71.

[6]Oswald H. Ganley and Gladys D. Ganley, *To Inform or to Control? The New Communications Networks*. New York, McGraw-Hill, 1982, pp. 60–64.

Anthony Smith, *The Geopolitics of Information. How Western Culture Dominates the World*. Oxford University Press, New York, 1980.

William H. Read, *America's Mass Media Merchants*. The Johns Hopkins University Press, Baltimore and London, 1976.

"Kaupe: U.S. Mart Dominates the World," *Variety*, November 28, 1984, p. 82, says the U.S. has 60% of the world video market.

[7]Joelle Stolz, "TV Captivates Algeria. Cultural Conflict as 'Dallas' Sweeps In," *World Press Review*, January 1983, p. 60.

Bangladesh. Personal communications.

Samuel G. Freedman, "French Minister Cites U.S. Cultural Influence," *The New York Times*, November 16, 1984, p. C-26.

Cynthia Stevens, "TV Talk: American Shows Popular with African TV-Watchers," *The Associated Press*, September 5, 1979 (NEXIS).

Elihu Katz, "Israel. A Second TV Channel?" *InterMedia*, July/September 1983, pp. 55–56.

Jeffrey Heller, "TV World; Israel and Jordan Achieve," *United Press International*, June 2, 1983 (NEXIS).

[8]"New Technologies Hoist 'Jolly Roger' Over Intellectual Property Worldwide," *International Networks*, Volume 3, Number 2, February 1985, p. 1.

[9]Advertisement for Worldvision Enterprises, Inc., *Variety*, January 23, 1985, pp. 55–56.

[10]Bangladesh. Personal communications.

[11]Allister Sparks, "The Call of Bop-TV," *Connections. World Communications Report*, Number 15, September 10, 1984, pp. 1–2.

Mark Gleeson, "Say Anti-Apartheid Films to Unspool In So. Africa Despite Government Ban," *Variety*, December 26, 1984, p. 29.

"S. Africa Blocks Bop-TV's Spillage Into White Areas." *Variety*, January 9, 1985, p. 148.

[12]German Democratic Republic. Personal communications.

Hazel Guild, "Allow Cable Hookup of Western TV in East German Burg," *Variety*, November 13, 1985, p. 1.

Flora Lewis, "The Dresden Paradigm," *The New York Times*, November 6, 1984, p. A-25. (Flora Lewis questions the cable installation.)

[13]Hazel Guild, "East German Nets Spice Up Offerings With Western Pics," *Variety*, January 23, 1985, p. 53.

[14]Elihu Katz, "Israel, A Second TV Channel?" *InterMedia*, July/September 1983, pp. 55–56.

Jeffrey Heller, "TV World; Israel and Jordan Achieve," *United Press International*, June 2, 1983 (NEXIS).

Benjamin Compaine. Personal communications.

[15]"Freedom-Loving Estonians Charge That Soviets Are Trying to Crush Their Culture," *The Christian Science Monitor*, November 23, 1984, p. 17.

Eastern Europe. Personal communications.

[16]Jeane-Baptiste Dossè Placca, " 'Is Togo Television Yours or Mine?' " *Index on Censorship*, 5/84, pp. 21–23.

[17]*Ibid.*, p. 21.

[18]Charles J. Hanley, "Today's Focus: In the Age of Khomeini, Tehran Moves at Half-Step," *The Associated Press*, November 23, 1982 (NEXIS), and others.

[19]Javed Jabbar, "Pakistan. A Cautious Welcome," *Inter Media*, July/September 1983, p. 65.

[20]Kenya. Personal communications.

[21]B. Jicinski, "The East Bloc's Market for Media Imports," *The Wall Street Journal*, September 19, 1984, p. 33.

[22]Victor E. Ragosine, "Tape Recording," *The Encyclopedia Americana*. Volume 26, Grolier Inc., Danbury, CT, 1982, p. 282.

[23]Haifaa Khalafallah, "The Arab Cassette Culture. An Underground Response to Censorship," *World Press Review*, April 1983, p. 60.

[24]Gladys D. Ganley, *The Political Impact of Audio and Videocassettes and Recorders in Iran and Pakistan*, unpublished manuscript, Fall 1985.

See also:

Dilip Hiro, *Iran Under the Ayatollahs*. Routledge & Kegan Paul, London, 1985, pp. 55, 64, 68–69, 70, 74, 76–77, 83–87.

Nikki R. Keddie, *Roots of Revolution. An Interpretive History of Modern Iran*. Yale University Press, New Haven, 1981, pp. 242, 251.

John D. Stempel, *Inside the Iranian Revolution*. Indiana University Press, Bloomington, 1981, pp. 45, 47, 109, 127, 174.

Asaf Hussain, *Islamic Iran. Revolution and Counter-Revolution*. Frances Pinter, London, 1985, pp. 61, 64, 117, 124, 127, 130.

Hamid Mowlana, "Technology Versus Tradition: Communication in the Iranian Revolution," *Journal of Communications*, Summer 1979, pp. 105–110.

Majid Tehranian, "Iran: Communication, Alienation, Revolution," *InterMedia,* Volume 7, Number 6, March 1979.

[25]Elaine Sciolino, "The Big Brother. Iraq Under Saddam Hussein," *The New York Times Magazine,* February 3, 1985, p. 24.

[26]Review of V. S. Naipaul's *Among the Believers,* in *The Economist,* February 6, 1982, p. 92.

[27]"Israelis Trying to Make a Dent in the Pirate Cassette Market," *Variety,* January 30, 1985, p. 77.

Martin Sieff, "Islamic March Tiptoes Into Turkey," *Insight,* March 3, 1986, p. 32.

[28]Karen Dawisha and Hélène Carrere D'Encausse, "Islam in the Foreign Policy of the Soviet Union: A Double-Edged Sword?" In *Islam in Foreign Policy.* Adeed Dawisha, Ed., Cambridge University Press, Cambridge, 1983, p. 174.

[29]Steven R. Weisman, "Further Bombings Expected in India," *The New York Times,* May 17, 1985, p. A-23.

[30]Haifaa Khalafallah, "The Arab Cassette Culture. An Underground Response to Censorship," *World Press Review,* April 1983, p. 60.

[31]"Torture," *Reuters,* February 15, 1983 (NEXIS).

Haifaa Khalafallah, "The Arab Cassette Culture. An Underground Response to Censorship," *World Press Review,* April 1983, p. 60.

[32]Haifaa Khalafallah, "The Arab Cassette Culture. An Underground Response to Censorship," *World Press Review,* April 1983, p. 60.

[33]*Ibid.*

For an extensive interview with Sheikh Imam, see:

Marilyn Booth, "Sheikh Imam The Singer: An Interview," *Index on Censorship,* Volume 14, Number 3, June 1985, pp. 18–21.

For one political confrontation, in Tunisia, see:

"Tunisia," *Index on Censorship,* Volume 13, Number 6, December 1984, pp. 48–49.

[34]Chris Kutschera, "Immigrants Take to the Air Waves," *The Middle East,* January 1985, p. 17.

[35]Haifaa Khalafallah, "The Arab Cassette Culture. An Underground Response to Censorship," *World Press Review,* April 1983, p. 60.

[36]*Ibid.*

[37]"Middle Eastern Story-tellers Give Way to Videos," *Index on Censorship,* Volume 14, Number 1, February 1985, p. 53.

[38]Unni Wikan, "Living Conditions Among Cairo's Poor — A View From Below," *The Middle East Journal,* Volume 39, Number 1, Winter 1985, p. 14.

[39]James Clad, "They Shall Not Pas," *Far Eastern Economic Review,* October 18, 1984, p. 17.

[40]"Malaysia," *Index on Censorship,* Volume 13, Number 6, December 1984, p. 46.

[41]*Ibid.*

[42]James Clad, "Malaysia Bans Islamic Tapes, American Books," *Far Eastern Economic Review,* January 8, 1985, p. 8.

[43]John Kifner, "Cultural Revolt Budding in Poland Despite Arrests," *The New York Times,* April 3, 1984, p. 1.

Bradley Graham, "Polish Resistance Flourishes Under Eyes of Regime," *The Washington Post,* November 26, 1983, p. A-1.

[44]John Kifner, "Cultural Revolt Budding in Poland Despite Arrests," *The New York Times,* April 3, 1984, p. 1.

[45]Jacek Kalabinski, "Media War in Poland: The Government vs. the Underground," *Poland Watch,* April 1984, p. 73.

For Bratkowski's description of his own activities, see:

Stefan Bratkowski, "We Cannot Surrender," *Index on Censorship,* October 1985, back cover.

For activities of the Polish underground publishing house, NOWa, which is putting plays, including a dramatized Orwell's *Nineteen Eighty-Four* and other political materials, on audiocassettes, see:

"In the World of Independent Culture," *Extracts From Polish Underground Publications,* Teresa Hanicka and Nika Krzeczunowicz, compilers and translators, RAD Polish Underground Extracts/8, *Radio Free Europe Research,* Radio Free Europe-Radio Liberty, May 21, 1985, pp. 3–9. Article originally from *Tygodnik Mazowsze,* Number 114, January 24, 1985.

"Fewer Setbacks, More Books: A Talk With the Independent Publishing House NOWa," *Extracts From Polish Underground Publications,* Teresa Hanicka and Nika Krzeczunowicz, compilers and translators, RAD Polish Underground Extracts/8, *Radio Free Europe Research,* Radio Free Europe-Radio Liberty, pp. 13–20. Article originally from *Vacat,* Number 17/18, May/June 1984.

Teresa Hanicka, "Underground Videotape Production," Situation Report, Poland/8, *Radio Free Europe Research,* Radio Free Europe-Radio Liberty, May 21, 1985, p. 23.

[46]Douglas Stanglin. Personal communications.

[47]Timothy Garton Ash, *The Polish Revolution. Solidarity.* Vintage Books, New York, 1985, pp. 46–47.

[48]"Israel Closes University Over Banned Materials," *The New York Times,* March 4, 1985, p. A-4.

[49]*Ibid.*

[50]*Ibid.*

"Cassettes of Palestinian music" were also reported to have been confiscated by Israeli troops in October 1983 from "a Palestinian folklore exhibition at Bethlehem University." See: "Index Index. Israel and the Occupied Territories." *Index on Censorship,* February 1984, p. 44. On April 19, 1985, Bethlehem University was "closed indefinitely" after a "search had revealed literature and tape cassettes containing Palestinian nationalist material." "Index Index. Israel and the Occupied Territories." *Index on Censorship,* October 1985, p. 66.

Confiscations of audiocassettes for political content have also been reported in Bahrain. "Index Index. Bahrain," *Index on Censorship,* December, 1985, p. 55.

[51]"Index Index. Ecuador," *Index on Censorship,* October, 1985, p. 65.

[52]"The Island Paradise That's Becoming a Communist Stronghold," *Business Week,* November 19, 1984, p. 66.

[53]*Ibid.*

[54]"Seychelles Screen-less," *Variety,* July 10, 1985, p. 92.

[55]"The Island Paradise That's Becoming a Communist Stronghold," *Business Week,* November 19, 1984, p. 66.

[56]*Ibid.,* and also:

Research Institute Recommendations, September 21, 1984, p. 4.

Richard Bernstein, "Mitterand Ends Visit to New Caledonia," *The New York Times,* January 20, 1985, p. A-3.

Robert Kaylor, "Storm Signals Fly for U.S. in South Pacific," *U.S. News & World Report,* March 4, 1985, pp. 31–33.

[57]Hamish McDonald, "Pacific Show of Force," *Far Eastern Economic Review,* January 24, 1985, pp. 10–11.

[58]Richard N. Ostling, "Billy Graham's Mission Improbable," *Time,* September 24, 1984, p. 48.

[59]Donald R. Shanor, *Behind the Lines. The Private War Against Soviet Censorship.* St. Martin's Press, New York, 1985, p. 159.

[60]James Brooke, "Listened to Any Good Books Lately?", *The New York Times,* July 2, 1985, p. C-9.

[61]Donald R. Shanor, *Behind the Lines,* pp. 159–160.

[62]*Ibid.,* p. 160.

[63]*Ibid.,* p. 160 for *Gulag,* pp. 6–7 for KAL 007.

[64]*Ibid.,* p. 161.

[65]*Ibid.,* pp. 161–162.

[66]Douglas Stanglin. Personal communications.

[67]Colin McIntyre, "Dateline: Gdansk, Poland," *Reuters Ltd.,* August 29, 1980, (NEXIS).

[68]"Customs Chief in Trouble with Religious Literature," *Newsletter From Behind the Iron Curtain. Reports on Communist Activities in Eastern Europe,* Volume 37, Number 517/518, Stockholm, July-October 1983, p. 20.

[69]"Soviet Spy Agency Reportedly Spreading Phony Reagan Tapes," *United Press International,* January 8, 1984 (NEXIS).

[70]*Ibid.*

[71]*Ibid.*

[72]*Ibid.*

[73]Gladys D. Ganley, *The Political Impact of Audio and Videocassettes and Recorders in Iran and Pakistan,* Unpublished manuscript, Fall 1985, p. 13.

John D. Stempel, *Inside the Iranian Revolution.* Indiana University Press, Bloomington, 1981, p. 174.

[74]Orville Schell, *To Get Rich is Glorious. China in the 80's.* Pantheon Books, New York, 1984, pp. 191–195.

[75]*Ibid.,* p. 193.

[76]Christopher S. Wren, "Off-Key or Off-Color, Tunes of West Worry China," *The New York Times,* October 28, 1982, p. A-2.

[77]*Ibid.*

[78]Liang Heng and Judith Shapiro, *Intellectual Freedom in China After Mao. With a Focus on 1983.* Fund for Free Expression Report, New York, 1984, pp. 156–157.

[79]Steven W. Mosher, *Broken Earth. The Rural Chinese.* The Free Press, New York, 1983, pp. 8, 84, 92, 93, 101–103, 134–136, 145, 160, 166, 185.

[80]*Ibid.,* pp. 8, 84, 92, 103, 145.

[81]*Ibid.,* p. 103.

[82]*Ibid.,* p. 185.

[83]"Index Index. Vietnam," *Index on Censorship,* Volume 15, Number 1, January 1986, p. 36.

CHAPTER THREE

The Hardware: VCR Penetration

Available statistics on VCR penetration are often guesses, for these machines frequently do not stay in the country to which they are shipped originally. *InterMedia* has pointed out that the VCR market is much more "informal and volatile" than the markets for TV, film, or telecommunications, which are both licensed and monitored. There are few countries, it says, where statistics are collected by any "regular" means, and what observers say often dramatically conflicts with the "official" trade figures:

> A major problem is the extent of illegal trade. Many VCRs travel through several countries, and even change their brand names, before finding a home. For instance, about three-quarters of VCR imports into the United Arab Emirates are re-exported, many of them to Iran where there is no recognized video market. Even where trade is legal, difference in prices (as between, say, the UK and Ireland) encourage people to go shopping across the border and bring back a VCR that will never appear in the official statistics.[1]

Three figures included as Appendix B demonstrate some of the variations in reported VCR penetration figures, as do data included in Appendix A.* Figure 1, for instance, shows that, if the number of VCRs — 387,809 — shipped to Panama by Japanese manufacturers had stayed there, every Panamanian with a television** would have 1.76 VCRs. Figure 2 gives the estimated penetration of VCRs into Panama for 1983 as 82% of the homes with television, or about half the rate estimated in Figure 1. Figure 3 shows Panama with 50,000 VCRs, as does data personally communicated to the authors (see Appendix A). With an estimated 480,000 television receivers in Panama,[2] this would make VCR penetration around 10% of TVs. The real figure for Panama is probably not known. What is known is that, in this and many instances, vast numbers of VCRs entering one country are, legally or illegally, going elsewhere. One 1985 source says of the estimated 500,000 VCRs in Colombia, "most [have been] smuggled in from Panama. . . ."[3]

The government of Mexico, in a June 1982 austerity move, banned the import of luxury items, including videocassette recorders.[4] The VCR count then stood at about 180,000. In March 1985, the VCR count was estimated

---

* All figures are constantly being revised upward, as both actual numbers and available data change.

** According to the numbers of TVs in this figure.

to be between 450,000 and 500,000, although no VCRs had since been legally imported.[5] These illegal machines were said by one source to be mainly coming in over the U.S. border.[6]

The figures for VCR penetration into India also vary widely. Figure 1 shows that 76,765 VCRs had been shipped by Japan, by the end of 1983, to that country. *Reuters,*[7] in fall 1983, said India had 300,000 VCRs, with another 20,000 arriving monthly. In February 1984, *The New York Times* gave much the same information.[8] In fall 1984, one *Variety* article reported a 180,000 VCR count for India.[9] Figure 3, which is excerpted from another *Variety* article, shows the Indian VCR count to be 610,000. Meanwhile, personally communicated information indicates that VCRs are possessed by fewer than 100,000 Indian families.

Figure 1 shows the Cypriots with 136.21% VCR penetration,[10] Kuwait with 127.49%, the Maldives (a poor little island group off the coast of India and Sri Lanka with only 1000 to 1500 television sets)[11] with 106.50%, Oman with 124.99%, Singapore with 284.32%, the United Arab Emirates with 505.16%, and Zaire with 178.20%. While some inhabitants of the rich oil states may have a VCR "in every room,"[12] none of these figures is really credible for actual penetration. Many of these machines are siphoned off illegally (as well as, of course, legally) to other places. Dubai, United Arab Emirates, for instance, is noted for "informal" re-exportation of large quantities of luxury and consumer goods to its more restricted neighbors, including Iran and Saudi Arabia.[13]

At the very least, in countries where freedom to own a VCR is not at issue, taxes as well as registration, which can lead to annual rather steep fees, are imposed but are routinely avoided. In France, for instance, consideration was given to dropping the annual VCR fee, scheduled to be 641 francs, or $71 in 1985. *Variety* commented, "loss of revenue from the annual fee should not cause major upset since most VCR owners dodge paying the fee anyway."[14] Europeans already pay hefty fees for television licenses,[15] which are used in lieu of advertising to offset some of the costs of programming.

Many countries attempt to exact taxes from VCR imports and sales. Spain has a 24% import duty on VCRs and a 20% luxury tax on video sales.[16] When VCRs were finally permitted into Tanzania (they were banned until June 1983), they were both taxed and an annual license fee of about 50 pounds (British) imposed.[17] Turkey has permitted VCRs to come in, but has put high duties on these and other imported products, hoping to use the funds to finance low cost housing. It is unclear how much of this money is being collected.[18] Pakistan has a 100% import duty on VCRs.[19] Denmark has a $380 tax on a $950 VCR.[20] Israel already had a 50% duty on VCRs[21] before a six-month ban was laid on VCR and other luxury imports.[22] On the other hand, Nepal, which has no television, has lowered duties on VCRs, either to encourage imports or to discourage illegal entry.[23] In Kuwait, both VCRs and cassettes are free of taxes.[24]

While researching *The Journeyer,* bestselling author Gary Jennings retraced the footsteps of Marco Polo. To get from Pakistan into Afghanistan, he says:

> "I bribed my way into a camel caravan of smugglers. . . . Some of the romance rubbed off . . . because you would think a desert caravan would be smuggling spices, perfumes and slave girls. Do you know what they were carrying? They had Sonys and VCRs dangling on the humps of camels."[25]

Some of these VCRs or others like them would undoubtedly find their way, with all sorts of other forbidden goods, across the USSR border. Despite the Soviet invasion of Afghanistan, many of the traditional units which have been smuggling for decades or even centuries are still in operation in Afghanistan, and VCRs and cassettes are among their hot new trade items.[26] To get Afghans to accept Soviet goods and services, "bartering across the border is encouraged — an Afghan horse for a Soviet refrigerator, for example. . . ."[27] It is easy to see that the flow of technology could also go in the opposite direction.

Smuggled VCRs and videotapes have been flooding into Bulgaria at a rate which is posing "a very real threat to the regime's censorship,"[28] says a *Radio Free Europe Research* report:

> The number of private video sets is growing alarmingly from the authorities' point of view, and they are becoming increasingly upset at being unable to control what is being watched at home by people with access to video equipment.[29]

A source for Eastern Europe[30] confirmed the steady growth of VCRs in Bulgaria described by *Radio Free Europe Research,* and added that, while the same situation may not yet prevail throughout all Eastern Europe, this is definitely the future pattern. Asked to rank the progress in VCR penetration in Eastern Europe by country, this source said Bulgaria is definitely number one, but that Hungary is close to, or perhaps even with, it. Czechoslovakia and East Germany are either right next to, or very close behind, Bulgaria. In short, they all are, or soon will be, more or less even.

Radio Free Europe Research and other sources show VCR penetration into Eastern Europe to be growing rapidly. *The Associated Press* reported that, at the beginning of 1985, there were from 20,000 to 30,000 VCRs in Hungary.[31] *Radio Free Europe Research* apparently accepted this number, but said that it had grown to 70,000 by June, and "was expected to increase to 100,000" during the summer.[32] This source also reported 70,000 VCRs in

Poland as early as 1984 — up from less than 3000 in 1983. Many of these are owned by clubs and parishes that make group showings.[33] In January 1986, *World Press Review,* citing the *Times* of London, gave a Polish VCR penetration figure of 150,000.[34]. Although a personal contact has said that "I estimate fewer than 2000 households have VCRs" in Czechoslovakia (see Appendix A), *Radio Free Europe Research,* admitting that "no reliable figures exist," says it has seen media estimates of VCRs smuggled into that country ranging from "a few thousand" to "more than 20,000."[35]

Although VCRs are not available for zlotys in Poland, they can be had at prices quite competitive with those in the West at the Polish dollar stores. There is a lot of money (zlotys) in Poland, especially among private entrepreneurs, says this source, but very little to spend it on, the one big exception being a house in the country.[36] This is also true in other Eastern European nations. So zlotys get turned into dollars via the black market (see Chapter 4) and become available for VCR and other consumer and luxury purchases. A very usual thing is also for three or four young couples to pool their money to buy a VCR which they can each use for periods of a week or two.[37] Political groups in Poland have their own VCR equipment. They have sometimes videotaped interviews with underground leaders to pass to the Western news media.[38] So does the underground publishing house, NOWa, and other groups, who are beginning to produce their own videotaped programming (see Chapter 5).

The penetration of VCRs into the Soviet Union is said by *Radio Free Europe Research*[39] to be, to date, "pre-embryonic" as compared to the situation in the countries of Eastern Europe. The supply of VCRs there is still quite small.[40] A 1982 article in *The Boston Globe* said, "It is not known how many video sets are in use in the Soviet Union, but sources suggest that there are only a few thousand."[41] *Time,* at the end of 1982, said that "there are about 50,000 privately owned VCRs in the U.S.S.R. . . ."[42] The highest number of VCRs seen for the USSR during this study was 60,000. *Variety,* in early 1986, gave the source of this figure as the Executive Director of the International Film Exchange (IFEX).[43] Several personal contacts were queried on this subject, but all declined to hazard guesses. Some privileged Soviet travelers have permission to buy and bring back a VCR, but these are few in number.[44] Official artists are the most privileged group in Russia. They can travel abroad, and this automatically means that they can get various Western consumer goods, which they bring in one way or another.[45] Soviet diplomats are another source of VCRs. According to Donald Shanor,

a certain discount jeans store a few blocks south of the United Nations on Manhattan's East Side has long been a favorite shopping place for Soviet diplomats and their families about to return home or go on leave. Now the electronics shops in the neighborhood and in midtown are getting business from the same clientele. They can buy the kind of video that will never be shown in the Soviet Union for twenty or thirty dollars, and a VCR for a tenth of the black market price in Moscow. Border controls do not constitute much of a problem for official travelers.[46]

Foreign businessmen sometimes "sweeten deals" with Soviet officials with gift VCRs, but the KGB is vigorously cracking down on this.[47] The Soviets are very worried that videocassettes will be used, as audiotapes are used, for "magnitizdat."* But the Soviet population is highly skilled in treading its way through bureaucratic and police controls.[49] There is a certain "sloppiness" that gives some leeway. There are also payoffs. Customs can, in some instances, be "fixed."[50]

Some Soviets have access to hard-currency tourist and diplomatic stores, and some spend their excess travel currency there rather than reconverting it.[51] *Variety* said in early 1986 that those with access to such hard currency shops could buy a VCR for "approximately half" what it would cost in local currency, the local currency cost being given as about "the equivalent of $1,600. . . ."[52] VCRs are also available at state-run commission stores — the so-called "second-hand" stores — where individuals can sell on consignment.[53] At those stores specializing in audio and television equipment, VCRs are said to be seen quite frequently, with even a few of the multisystem VCRs now appearing. The price given by this source was in the range of 2500 to 3000 rubles, or about $4000 for a regular PAL TV and VCR system, and, for a multisystem TV/multisystem VCR, about 9000 rubles, or $12,000.[54] This would amount to several years of salary for most Russians.

The figures are deceptive, however. In Russia, "middle- to upper-middle-income Soviet families (two or more earners) . . . have quite large discretionary incomes." This is partly because many essentials, such as medical care, education, housing, transportation, and utilities are either free or highly subsidized. A family earning 400 to 600 rubles a month pays 10 to 15 rubles for an apartment, or about 20, counting telephone and electricity.[55] Another source says for Russia, "while wages have been rising, the availability of consumer products has not kept pace. There is so little to buy and so much money chasing it that private savings accounts have burgeoned. . . ."[56] (See Chapter 4 for other discussions of global discretionary income.)

The Soviet Union has made an attempt to manufacture its own VCRs which has not, however, been very successful.[57] A limited number of VCRs have been made at the Elektronika factory at Voronezh. The USSR had

---

* "Samizdat" is the word for underground political print publications in the Soviet Union. "Magnitizdat" has been coined for the same sort of "tape publishing."[48]

hoped also to export some machines to Eastern European countries. But these VCRs have not gone over well with Soviet citizens. The units must be bought in Voronezh, and returned there for repairs. In addition, they do not operate on Western cassette standards, and do not have recording capability. Their price—about $1500, as compared to the $5000+ for smuggled Western and Japanese VCRs—is very reasonable. But the public is not enthusiastic, and, so far as sales go, the experiment has been a failure. *The New York Times* reported in December, 1985, however, that Soviet machines are now convertible, saying

> Soviet video players and television sets are not compatible with American, Japanese or most Western European models. The Soviet equipment, however, can be converted to handle movies recorded for other video systems, and a prospering underground business has developed to do just that, according to Moscovites. They said it costs about 400 rubles to have a Soviet color television converted.[58]

Since there is a large price advantage to buying a Soviet model, the future may see sales increasing. The Soviet government plans to speed up production of the Elektronika, saying it will produce "60,000 video players a year by 1990 and 120,000 a year by 2000."[59] The USSR is also said to have arranged with Hitachi to produce domestic SECAM VCRs in VHS format. Russia is cited as claiming to have produced 50,000 VCRs this way in 1984, and as saying it would produce 350,000 more in 1985.[60] A different source said

> last year the Soviets signed a pact with Panasonic for the in-country production of 10,000 players a year, a number that will grow to about 60,000 by 1990.[61]

All of this appears to be part of an "if you can't lick 'em, join 'em" effort to get a handle on this out-of-control information.

Czechoslovakia is attempting, in cooperation with Philips, to produce a domestic VCR, but the units are few in number so far and very expensive.[62] Hungary's Orion enterprise is also cooperating with Japan's Panasonic, but will produce only about 1000 units annually.[63] Personal VCRs are being permitted to enter Hungary under certain circumstances, and the customs duty has actually been lowered.[64] This is occurring as Hungary and other Eastern European countries, along with the USSR, are attempting to produce or distribute their own approved programming (see Chapters 4 and 10).

Movies are an absolute passion with the Indians, who make more than 700 a year in a dozen languages, and export a lot of them. Indians will go to the cinema, then go home and watch a movie on television, and then hook up their VCRs and watch again.[65] While the intelligentsia may tend to look down on the movie as an inferior art, "the masses developed a passion for [it] finding in it an instant escape medium in which to forget the drudgery of daily life. . . ."[66] Officially, India protects its economy from imports, but smuggled goods are to be found everywhere, including one of Bombay's busiest thoroughfares. These goods are said to be off-loaded nightly from dhows from Dubai, in "the thousands of coves and inlets that dot the rocky coastline near [Bombay]."[67] If the duties were paid, a top-brand video-cassette recorder would have cost an Indian about $9000 in 1982. From smugglers, it could be had for half that cost. This is a VCR that would sell in Dubai or Singapore for about $1600.[68]

Another source of VCRs and other consumer items in India is a hard-currency duty-free shopping complex which Sri Lanka runs in Colombo. Here

> prices are so attractive that merchants . . . in Madras and Bombay send "couriers" to buy for them. The merchant gets the courier a passport and return ticket, and gives him dollars and a shopping list. After his Sri Lankan shopping spree, the courier gets a commission and the merchant sells the goods at a large profit. . . . The planes from Madras are always full, the ferry from India is booked months in advance. Trains from the ferry to Colombo are packed with India couriers armed with gunnysacks [to carry their purchases]. . . .[69]

Such items coming in from "free ports" are said to usually be sold through the black market.[70] Sri Lankans are not permitted in these stores without hard currency.[71]

Dhows from Dubai also smuggle consumer and luxury items into Iran, which became a number one customer for such "transshipments" following the Khomeini revolution. Iranians pay for these goods with "carpets, works of art and cash they probably are withdrawing from mattresses and other hiding places. . . ."[72] Although the export of carpets is the sole prerogative of the Iranian government, thousands find their way to the Arab Emirates.[73] Bazaar merchants, who originally supported Khomeini but became dissatisfied with the results of the revolution, took advantage via the black market of "stiff foreign-exchange controls and other trade regulations" to make huge profits on VCRs and "whatever the marketplace wanted."[74]

The figures cited for VCR penetration into China vary widely (see Figures 1, 2, and 3 in Appendix B). A *Variety* article, in fall 1985, gave it as 800,000.[75] This is 13.3 times the highest figure (60,000) seen for the Soviet Union, although China has only about four times the Soviet Union's population. Chinese VCR figures are increasing rapidly, due, among other things, to gifts from overseas Chinese and, especially, to smuggling (see Chapter 4). Recently, contracts have also been made by the Chinese with Japanese companies to produce some VCRs locally.[76]

VCR penetration is high, especially in urban areas, in many of the countries of Asia and the Pacific Basin. It is very high in the Middle East. It is just getting going in many countries of South America, and, with a few exceptions, is still quite low in Africa. Some VCRs have, however, penetrated into even the smallest and poorest countries. And everywhere, globally, despite any restrictions, their numbers are seen to be steadily growing.

Varying broadcast and VCR hardware standards have created large but obviously not insurmountable difficulties. Multistandard TV sets have been popular in Saudi Arabia since the early 1970s, where

> Sony has been a leader in selling multicolor and multiline system(s). . . .
> These receivers are still popular because they are used with multisystem VCRs and because in the Eastern Province of the kingdom viewers may receive the two Saudi channels on both the German PAL and French SECAM systems. Neighboring states (Kuwait, Qatar, and the U.A.E.) transmit in PAL color.[77]

Multisystem VCRs which could play PAL, SECAM, and American tapes satisfactorily became available from Hitachi only in 1984, although other companies are now providing them. Prior to this, Europeans had recourse to the JVC, which would play PAL and SECAM, but American tapes only on the fastest speeds.[78] For the Russians, Western and Japanese machines could be converted only very expensively.[79] Such incompatibilities had interesting political implications in Russia, however, since they led to widespread trading back and forth of tapes, causing much social networking.[80]

Two major global forces have been seen to be implicated in the rapid VCR distribution past borders that, in theory, should be more impervious. One is the wide existence of secondary, or black market, economies which are necessary to keep dozens of nations functioning. The other is a vast migrant labor pool involving millions of people and many countries. This migrant labor must, to some extent, be placated by governments, because the economies of many nations have become dependent upon remittances from it. Remittance economies and black market economies often exist simultaneously, making it even more difficult for would-be restrictive governments to keep the kind of control they might like to keep over what passes across their borders.

NOTES

[1]"Video Cassette Recorders: National Figures," *InterMedia*, July/September 1983, p. 38.

[2]"South 120. The Third World At Your Fingertips. Panama," *South*, October 1984 (pages unnumbered).

[3]Peter Besas, " 'Legal' Homevid in Latino Orbit. Huge Potential From a New Territory," *Variety*, March 20, 1985, p. 61.

[4]Paul Lenti, "Televisa Enters Latin Homevid Arena Creating New Local Businesses," *Variety,* March 20, 1985, p. 91.

[5]*Ibid.,* and also:

"Odd Saga of Mexican Homevid. How It Came to Pass that VCRs and Videocassettes Became Smugglers' Items," *Variety,* March 20, 1985, p. 96.

[6]Steve Frazier, "A Slum Black Market in Mexico Is a Part of the Establishment," *The Wall Street Journal,* March 25, 1985, p. 1.

[7]Francis Daniel, "Dateline: Singapore," *Reuters,* September 24, 1983 (NEXIS).

[8]William K. Stevens, "Bazaars of India are Now a Toyland of High Tech," *The New York Times,* February 2, 1984, p. A-2.

[9]"S.E. Asia VCR Count," *Variety,* October 10, 1984, p. 37.

[10]When Benjamin Compaine of this Program visited Cyprus in Fall 1984, he was told that VCR penetration there was about 40%. Benjamin Compaine. Personal communications.

[11]"South 120. The Third World at Your Fingertips. Maldives," *South,* October 1984 (pages unnumbered).

[12]Joan Borsten, "Drilling for Dollars in Movie-Mad Kuwait," *The Los Angeles Times, Calendar,* March 11, 1984, p. 21.

In a 1986 special report by *The Economist,* it was said of the Persian Gulf Area, "It is not uncommon for a house to have five video recorders. . . ." Home movies substitute for a lack of almost all other entertainment in some Gulf countries, including cinemas, theater, bars, restaurants, mixed male–female gatherings, and reading. "Growing Pains. The Gulf Co-operation Council Countries. A Survey." *The Economist,* February 8, p. 14 of Special Section following p. 52 of this issue.

[13]Ray Vicker, "Dubai's Traders Are Building a Thriving Trade Smuggling Goods Into Iran," *The Wall Street Journal,* May 7, 1980, p. 48. Reprinted as "Dubai's Enterprising Traders Smuggle Goods Into Iran" in Burgess Laughlin, *Black Markets Around The World,* Loompanics Unlimited, Mason, MI, 1981, pp. 35–37.

[14]"French Official Tells Vidcom-ers He Backs Abolition of VCR Fee," *Variety,* October 17, 1984, p. 38.

[15]"The Prince of TV in Europe," *Variety,* October 17, 1984, p. 98.

[16]"Spanish Home Vid Facts and Figures," *Variety,* October 10, 1984, p. 39.

[17]Ludovick A. Ngatara, "Tanzania. Economy Down, Video up," *InterMedia,* July/September 1983, p. 71.

[18]Steven Erlanger, "A Supply-Sider in Turkey," *The Boston Globe,* October 14, 1984, p. A-89.

[19]Javed Jabbar, "Pakistan. A Cautious Welcome," *InterMedia,* July/September, 1983, pp. 65–66.

[20]"Levy Stalls Sales of Danish VCR's," *Variety,* October 10, 1984, p. 108.

[21]"Homevid Rental Fees in Slump After Israel Economic Downturn," *Variety,* October 10, 1984, p. 80.

[22]Yuval Elizur, "6-month Import Ban on Cars, Other Items Imposed in Israel," *The Boston Globe,* October 4, 1984, p. 4.

[23]Nepal. Personal communications.

[24]Sohair A. Barakat, "Kuwait. Video Land," *InterMedia,* July/September, 1983, p. 61.

[25]Jim Lewis, "An Author's Quest of Marco Polo," *United Press International,* January 24, 1984 (NEXIS).

[26]The Soviet Union. Personal communications.

[27]Christina Dameyer, "In Campaign to 'Sovietize' Afghanistan, USSR Uses School, Media, and Ethnic Ties," *The Christian Science Monitor,* March 26, 1985, p. 9.

[28]G. S., "Bulgaria Goes Into the Video Business," Situation Report, Bulgaria/13, *Radio Free Europe Research,* Radio Free Europe-Radio Liberty, October 10, 1984, p. 4.

[29]*Ibid.*, p. 3.

[30]Eastern Europe. Personal communications.

Variety reported in February 1986 that "it's estimated there are about 100,000. . . ." VCRs in Hungary. David Stratton, "No Standouts At Hungaro Week, Pics Reflect Industry's Malaise," *Variety*, February 19, 1986, p. 7. This article also said "officials are aware of a good deal of smuggling from the West, including porno movies and 'Rambo: First Blood Part II,' which is worse than porno in the eyes of many" (p. 400).

[31]George Jahn, "Video Cassette Black Market Flourishes in Hungary," *The Associated Press,* April 26, 1985 (NEXIS).

[32]Steven Koppany, "Unprepared Regime Scrambles to Meet Challenges of the Video Era," Situation Report, Hungary/10, *Radio Free Europe Research,* Radio Free Europe-Radio Liberty, September 4, 1985, p. 17.

[33]Teresa Hanicka, "Underground Video Tape Production," Situation Report, Poland/8, *Radio Free Europe Research,* Radio Free Europe-Radio Liberty, May 21, 1985, p. 23.

[34]"Early Warning, Miscellany," *World Press Review,* January 1986, p. 7.

[35]V. S., "On the Verge of the Video Revolution," Situation Report, Czechoslovakia/9, *Radio Free Europe Research*, Radio Free Europe-Radio Liberty, June 3, 1985, p. 31.

[36]Douglas Stanglin. Personal communications.

[37]*Ibid.*

[38]*Ibid.*

[39]G. S., "Bulgaria Goes Into the Video Business," Situation Report, Bulgaria/13, *Radio Free Europe Research*, Radio Free Europe-Radio Liberty, October 10, 1984, pp. 1–5.

[40]*Ibid.*

[41]John Miller, "The Latest Threat to Soviet Society," *The Boston Globe,* November 8, 1982, p. 1. Reprinted from the *London Daily Telegraph.*

[42]"VCRs Go on Fast Forward: Proliferating Player and Tapes Spread Western Fare Worldwide," *Time,* December 13, 1982, p. 78.

[43]James Melanson, "Soviets Crack A Window for U.S. Homevideo, But Floods of Rubles Unlikely," *Variety,* January 22, 1986, p. 16.

[44]The Soviet Union. Personal communications.

[45]*Ibid.*

[46]Donald R. Shanor, *Behind the Lines. The Private War Against Soviet Censorship.* St. Martin's Press, New York, 1985, p. 157.

[47]The Soviet Union. Personal communications.

Among the many articles that discuss the Russian situation are:

Ned Temko, "Kremlin Sees Threat in Uncensored Videocassettes," *The Christian Science Monitor,* May 12, 1983, p. 2.

Serge Schmemann, "Video's Forbidden Offerings Alarm Moscow," *The New York Times,* October 22, 1983, p. A-1.

Alison Smale, "Soviets Battle Black Market in Western Movie Cassettes," *Philadelphia Inquirer,* April 10, 1983, p. I-5.

Philip Taubman, "Oh Comrade, Can I Borrow Your Rambo Cassette?" *The New York Times,* December 9, 1985, p. A-2.

[48]Donald R. Shanor, *Behind the Lines. The Private War Against Soviet Censorship.* St. Martin's Press, New York, 1985, p. 159.

[49]The Soviet Union. Personal communications.

[50]*Ibid.*

[51]*Ibid.*

[52]James Melanson, "Soviets Crack a Window for U.S. Home Video, But Flood of Rubles Unlikely," *Variety,* January 22, 1986, p. 16.

[53]The Soviet Union. Personal communications.

[54]*Ibid.*

[55]Ian Menzies, "A Letter from Moscow. Impressions of Daily Life Tend to Push Aside Thoughts of Ideology." *The Boston Globe,* August 27, 1984, p. 2.

[56]Richard Anderson, "Economy Gorbachev's Priority," *The Boston Globe,* March 17, 1985, p. A-21.

[57]"VCRs That Will Spout the Party Line," *Business Week,* September 3, 1984, p. 40.

Elisa Tinsley, "Soviet Union Sets Stage for Video Revolution, United Press International, September 9, 1984 (NEXIS).

Elisa Tinsley, "Soviets Finally Get Tapes For Their VCRs," *USA Today,* December 6, 1985, p. A-4.

[58]Philip Taubman, "Oh Comrade, Can I Borrow Your Rambo Cassette?" *The New York Times,* December 9, 1985, p. A-2.

[59]*Ibid.*

[60]John Chittock, "Russia Moves to Exploit Video," *Financial Times* of London, March 19, 1985.

[61]James Melanson, "Soviets Crack A Window for U.S. Home Video, But Flood of Rules Unlikely," *Variety,* January 22, 1986, p. 16.

[62]V. S., "On the Verge of the Video Revolution," Situation Report, Czechoslovakia/9, *Radio Free Europe Research,* Radio Free Europe-Radio Liberty, June 3, 1985, p. 31.

[63]Steven Koppany, "Unprepared Regime Scrambles to Meet Challenges of the Video Era," Situation Report, Hungary/10, *Radio Free Europe Research,* Radio Free Europe-Radio Liberty, September 4, 1985, p. 21.

[64]*Ibid.*

[65]T. N. Ninan and Chander Uday Singh, "India's Entertainment Revolution. A National Love Affair With Videocassettes," *World Press Review,* September 1983, p. 58.

See also:

Mary Anne Weaver, "India's Film Dandies Delight the Masses and Relieve Hard Lives," *The Christian Science Monitor,* November 28, 1983, p. 1.

[66]Paramesh Krishnan Nair, "India. It's Never Too Late . . . " *UNESCO Courier,* August 1984, pp. 22–23.

[67]Stuart Auerbach, "Smugglers Thrive in Protectionist India," *The Washington Post,* July 21, 1982, p. A-19.

[68]*Ibid.*

[69]John Worrall, "Indians Flock to Sri Lanka for Bargains," *The Christian Science Monitor,* April 5, 1983, p. 19.

[70]Stuart Auerbach, "Smugglers Thrive in Protectionist India," *The Washington Post,* July 21, 1982, p. A-19.

[71]John Worrall, "Indians Flock to Sri Lanka for Bargains," *The Christian Science Monitor,* April 5, 1983, p. 19.

[72]Ray Vicker, "Dubai's Traders Are Building a Thriving Trade Smuggling Goods Into Iran," *The Wall Street Journal,* May 7, 1980, p. 48. Reprinted as "Dubai's Enterprising Traders Smuggle Goods Into Iran," in Burgess Laughlin, *Black Markets Around the World,* Loompanics Unlimited, Mason, MI, 1981, p. 36.

[73]*Ibid,* p. 37.

Kathy Bishtawi, "TV Talk: Illicit Video Thrives in Conservative Gulf," *The Associated Press,* April 29, 1981 (NEXIS).

[74]Terry Povey, "Back to the Bazaar," *The Middle East,* April, 1983, p. 8.

[75]"China Nears Agreement With Western Producers Over Video Copyrights," *Variety,* October 23, 1985, pp. 1, 84.

[76]"China's Technology Imports Double Pace," *The Xinhua General Overseas News Service,* August 18, 1985 (NEXIS).

[77]Douglas A. Boyd and Joseph D. Straubhaar, "Developmental Impact of the Home Video Cassette Recorder on Third World Countries," *Journal of Broadcasting & Electronic Media,* Volume 29, Number 1, Winter 1985, p. 19.

[78]The Soviet Union. Personal communications.

[79]*Ibid.*

[80]*Ibid.*

CHAPTER FOUR

The Role of the Black Market in VCR Penetration

In many countries around the world, smuggling is just one arm of a fully mature black market which includes tax evasion, illegal speculation, black currency financing, and a host of other things which form an economy parallel to the official one.[1]

In the 1940s, Guenter Reimann described black market development in countries with strictly controlled economies.[2] Black markets, he said, develop in three stages: first, they are prohibited by the state; second, they are tolerated by the state; and third, they become indispensible to the state and thus come to be "authorized" or "legalized." During short term economic difficulties in unrestricted economies, black markets usually remain within the first or second stages. But they mature to the third stage in strictly controlled economies where shortages become permanent and relief for citizens is not to be had otherwise. Mr. Reimann says

> the black market . . . is not a deliberate creation of the state planners. It settles in the crevices of the structure of regimentation and finally becomes an integral part of the national economy.[3]

The black market situation in Burma was recently described in almost the same words by a professor of political science at Rutgers University. In 1962, "a small group of military leaders seized power and directed the [Burmese] nation down an uncharted road to socialism. . . ."[4] The few existing industries and commercial enterprises were nationalized, and farmers were directed to sell their produce to the state, which would be the sole exporter. The government "took measures that broke the economic power of Indian shopkeepers, traders and other businessmen. . . ."[5] This was temporarily popular. Then soldiers took over manufacture and distribution, which rapidly broke down:

> In this situation, a parallel black market economy arose to supply the needs and wants of the people. Initially, the military sought to stamp out its economic rival, but gradually the government came to realize that it could not fill the gap and the black market became a permanent fixture in Burmese economic life. . . .[6]

33

The Burmese black market is now estimated to be anywhere from one-fourth to more than one-half the size of the legal economy.[7] On this market, "the Burmese in Rangoon or other large towns can obtain virtually anything — from a small pin to a Japanese video-cassette recorder. . . ."[8] Much of the black market material comes in across the Thai border — frequently transported by elephant[9] — but electronics from Singapore often enter through southern Burmese ports. Smuggling routes also crisscross Burma, into and out of China, Bangladesh, and India.[10]

S. K. Ray described the early 1970s black market situation in India in which smugglers

> maintain[ed] their own wireless systems, speed boats, convoys of trucks, jeeps and motorcars with fictitious number plates and a local army of aides and helpers all over the country. They . . . spread their tentacles over business houses, industries, share markets, motion pictures, construction industries and other walks of life with impunity. They . . . built multi-storyed buildings and palaces for themselves, using their resources derived from smuggling. This is true of many countries.[11]

This Indian situation still exists. In 1982, an estimated $7 billion worth of goods, or half the amount of India's legal imports, were smuggled in annually.[12] VCRs, as the newest status symbol, are best-selling items on this voluminous black market.

The Soviet Union and the countries of Eastern Europe all have highly advanced black markets. *Time* says

> the Kremlin grudgingly accepts the underground economy because it fills the gaps left in the inefficient Soviet system, eases shortages and makes consumers' lives bearable. Collective-farm managers admit that often the only way to meet their production targets is to buy supplies on the black market. "If they tried to shut down every illegal activity," says one Western diplomat in Moscow, "the economy would come close to collapsing and the party would face serious problems of public disorder." The underground economy is nowhere to be found in the theories of Marx or Lenin, but it has become an integral part of Soviet society today.[13]

Again, VCRs are among the most wanted black market items. In 1983, *The Christian Science Monitor,* among others, reported on black market prices for VCRs in the USSR.[14]

An interesting feature of the black market in Eastern Europe and the Soviet Union is the existence of so called "bursas." This name for the stock exchange, says *The Wall Street Journal,* "has come to mean secret trading in free ideas: prohibited or officially unobtainable books, magazines, records and tape recordings. . . ."[15] These bursas exist from the "back alleys to the parks and woodlands of . . . far suburbs. . . ."[16] in all the big cities of the Soviet Union and Eastern Europe:

> Just about every self-respecting big city east of the Berlin Wall has a bursa. To avoid police confiscation of goods, the bursas in the U.S.S.R. have no merchandise — only book titles, lists, traders' addresses and prices.[17]

Both traders and customers learn about the irregularly held markets, which shift from place to place, via the underground grapevine. There are specialists for everything. Many items come into the black market from censors who, instead of censoring them, " 'just steal them and sell them on the black market' . . . ."[18]

Forbes, in 1984, explained how Poland, for one, accommodates itself to the necessities of the black market.[19] From the early 1960s onward, it has been issuing scrip called bons, which maintain the same value as the U.S. dollar, "at least on the black market."[20] According to *Forbes,*

> a Polish citizen cannot take 1 bon to the bank and freely get 1 U.S. dollar for it. That has to be done on the black market. But a citizen can take his U.S. dollar to the bank and exchange it for a bon.[21]

Bons can also be bought with zlotys at the black market rate. And bons, unlike zlotys, but like hard currencies, can be spent at state-run Pewex stores to buy VCRs and other otherwise unobtainable items.[22] The Polish government helpfully puts out a 19-page weekly bulletin called VETO, which

> carries a black market price index for both the U.S. dollar and gold. Not in so many words, of course. The unofficial zlotys-per-dollar rate is simply inferred from the quoted rate on legally traded bons.[23]

Another source has confirmed this use of bons in Poland.[24] In the early '80s, while the official exchange rate was 100 zlotys/dollar, the black market rate was 750 zlotys/dollar. People in Poland who legally run private businesses make a lot of zlotys, and there is nothing to buy with them. So they turn them into bons/dollars, via the black market, and use them to buy dollar-store items. VCRs can be had in the dollar store for not much more than the cost in Sweden.[25] This is because the dollar stores buy in bulk and do not have to pay the high taxes usually imposed on VCRs. It is legal to have dollars, because large numbers of Poles have relatives outside the country who send them money, and also because many Poles work abroad, where they can earn dollars. The Polish government encourages the influx of such hard currency. Poles, however, are reluctant to put their dollars in banks, because a constantly changing legal situation makes it uncertain that they can withdraw them.[26]

In fall 1982, the Yugoslav government took austerity measures, limiting gasoline to 10 gallons a month and imposing an $80 deposit fee on a trip out of the country. The result:

> Virtually everyone has his own special contacts with the black marketeers. . . . Dusko Radovic, who conducts a popular radio program called "Good Morning Belgrade!" remarked, "Actually the Government should award medals to the black marketeers for supplying the goods to the people that the Government isn't capable of supplying them."[27]

Nigeria has a big black market. *The New York Times* says

> smuggling is big business in Nigeria, a trade that embraces life's necessities and luxuries alike. It is said that for a $10,000 bribe, a customs official will busy himself elsewhere when a person of influence wants a container cleared at the port . . . A whole market on the road to Badagria specializes in smuggled electronic goods: hi-fi's, video machines and portable generators. . . .[28]

Black markets thrive under war conditions. In spring 1983, Lebanon began "a major crackdown on illegal imports. . . ."[29] On the very first day, "17 trucks and vans carrying videotape recorders, electrical supplies, vegetables and other food,"[30] worth about $1 million, were seized. The items other than vegetables (which came from Israel, through the Israeli-controlled part of Southern Lebanon) were either also from Israel, or from such illegal ports as Tripoli in Syrian-occupied Northern Lebanon. Control of illegal imports was expected to increase customs revenue five-fold, from the $100 million worth collected in 1982 to $500 million worth in 1983.[31] This effort was obviously not too successful, for, a year and a half later, the struggle against illegal imports was still in progress.[32]

In early 1984, among Syrian President Hafez Assad's alleged top priorities was the need to keep his army happy. One way they stayed happy was smuggling. Therefore

> the government, despite rigid austerity measures, looks the other way while soldiers smuggle fruit, American cigarettes, videocassettes and truckloads of building materials from Lebanon. A thriving underground economy is based on the large 'soldiers' market' in downtown Damascus, where military smugglers and black-market buyers meet.[33]

A crackdown during Ramadan in June 1984 is said to have greatly controlled smuggling by soldiers and border villagers. At its height, this was responsible for about 70% of the non-military imports of Syria, with up to $400,000 worth of illegal goods coming in daily. This included not only luxury goods (such as VCRs, etc.) but also raw materials to supply Syria's factories.[34]

Vietnamese raids on the Rithisen or Nong Samet refugee camp on the Thailand/Cambodian border, beginning at the end of 1984, not only caused thousands of civilians to flee into Thailand, but disrupted what had been "a major black market trading post supplying Thai and various foreign goods to the Cambodian interior, including Phnom Penh, the Vietnamese-held capital, and even to southern Vietnam."[35] VCRs and cassettes were part of the paraphernalia available at this camp.

In January 1985, a troubled North Vietnam was described 10 years after it "liberated" South Vietnam from Americans. Depending heavily on Soviet aid, it is said to be beset by debts, inflation, and wide shortages. It has, however, an active black market.[36] The black market also thrives in former Saigon, now Ho Chi Minh City:

> Black-market stalls that once were crammed with goods from U.S. post exchanges still operate openly in many of their old locations. Today the portable television sets and stereo tape recorders are smuggled in on ships from Singapore, Hong Kong, and other non-Communist ports. . . .[37]

A very interesting feature of this black market trade is that many of the customers are tourists and technicians from the Soviet-bloc nations.[38] Vietnamese buyers, again, include the farmers, who are now allowed to raise and sell pigs privately and have cash to buy TVs and other consumer items.[39]

In China, many peasants now have expendable income to buy luxuries like televisions and an occasional VCR, as a result of the "responsibility" system. But old money, in the form of millions of silver coins, has also entered black market circulation. These coins, issued between 1911, when the Republic of China was founded, and 1949, when the communist government took over, have been secreted away, and are now "being used to buy luxury consumer goods in the many black markets that have sprung up in the big cities since the recent liberalization of China's economic policy."[40] Chinese smugglers use the coins to barter for all sorts of electronic and other consumer goods with "fishermen" from Hong Kong, who meet them on the high seas off China. The coins, worth about U.S. $9.80 each, are melted down into blocks in Hong Kong and sold to local jewelers or to foreigners. The Chinese also barter for electronics with gold bars and herbal medicines.

Although China claims to have controlled some of this private smuggling, it is suffering from increased smuggling by "factories, government offices and people's organizations. . . ."[41] During the first half of 1985, more than 1000 such instances were reported, 3.7 times more than in 1984.[42] This con-

traband was specifically said to include television sets and videotape recorders, as well as motor vehicles, motorcycles, "and other consumer durables."[43]
The Economist reported in August 1985:

> Since January, 1984, officials of China's southern island of Hainan have been
> exploiting the island's de facto status as a free-trade zone to go on an import
> binge — and create the largest corruption scandal since Mr. Deng Xiaoping
> embarked on changing China's economic management. The officials bor-
> rowed $1.5 billion from state banks (equivalent to twice the value of last year's
> agricultural output on the semi-tropical island); and bought $570m in
> blackmarket American currency. They spent a lot of this on foreign consumer
> goods, mostly Japanese, which they sold around the country at up to 300%
> mark-ups.[44]

Noting that this was "an interesting reminder of the large hidden savings
held by Chinese households" and that Hainan officials "pocketed $30m from
black marketeers," *The Economist* said "the booty included 89,000 motor vehicles, 2.9m television sets and 252,000 video-recorders."[45] *Time* said that, in
August 1985,

> *People's Daily* reported that Xiang Dong, an official in Yunan province, had
> used state funds to buy pornographic videotapes. At the same time, China's
> news agency, Xinhua, revealed that some Hainan officials had jointly embez-
> zled about $1.5 billion by importing large quantities of cars, TV sets, video re-
> corders and motorcycles and reselling them at higher prices at government
> expense.[46]

In an attempt to curb the smuggling, in October 1985 a regulation was

> jointly drawn up by the ministry of foreign economic relations and trade, the
> ministry of commerce and the state administration for import and export com-
> modities inspection. . . .[47]

in which it was required that "imported household-used electrical appliances" including TVs, cassette recorders, hi-fi equipment, and video recorders, be inspected within certain time limits and "before being offered for
sale. . . ."[48] Officially, the regulation was said to be aimed at

> safeguarding national economic rights and interests as well as consumers' in-
> terests, and preventing certain foreign firms from dumping outdated and de-
> fective goods onto the Chinese market. . . .[49]

Radio Free Europe Research reported, at the end of 1983, on some "enigmatic
sources of income" in Eastern Europe, saying "Bulgaria is a country in which

a worker earns an average of 200 leva . . . spends 400 leva, and deposits 500 leva in the bank. . . ."[50] It tells of a Prague correspondent for the Belgrade daily *Politika* who,

> after touring several Eastern European countries . . . wrote that "puzzling sums of money, the origin of which cannot be traced, were circulating throughout Eastern Europe, despite the fact that wages there generally were very modest."[51]

The reporter, Slavoljub Djukic, was said to attribute this "enigmatic" income in Czechoslovakia, Hungary, Poland, and Bulgaria to several things, including: two jobs, the unofficial one paying more than the official one; two or more family earners; subsidized living costs; the use of "social means of production (state owned equipment)" to make things to sell privately; operation of private businesses; special privileges; and bribes and corruption.[52] Black market money, which has "created many billionaires in Poland" was also specifically mentioned.[53] The stealing and selling of state goods and property in the USSR and Eastern Europe is regularly mentioned by many sources.

Drug money has become a source of expendable income used to buy such luxuries as TVs and VCRs in many countries. Cocaine brings Bolivia $1.6 billion annually, three times the income from tin, Bolivia's biggest legal export item. As a result,

> imported color-television sets, stereo and cars — all contraband shipments — are openly unloaded at Santa Cruz's bustling international airport. US $100 bills are common currency in the city's stores. And when Indian families come to missionary medical clinics for outpatient treatment, they peel off the payments from rolls of crisp dollar bills.[54]

The downtown Mexico City black market center, Tepito, claims its name means " 'I'll whistle for you.' " But the smugglers who operate there say they stay on good terms with the Mexican authorities "provid[ing] thousands of jobs, cement[ing] political loyalty to the ruling party and keep[ing] . . . thieves busy in a less violent line of work."[55] The smugglers claim to all belong to the Partido Revolucionario Institucional (PRI), Mexico's foremost political party. One smuggler is quoted as saying " . . . 'We're 100% with the party because they let us work. . . . If they need a good turnout at a rally we don't just send 100 people. We send 2,000 or 3,000 so they will notice us.' "[56] Tepito is described as "a quarter-mile stretch of Tenochitlan Street, crammed sidewalk to sidewalk with videotape recorders, microwave ovens, home computers, pirated videocassettes . . . "[57]

The quality, prices, and availability in Tepito are said to be better than those for products made by the highly protected Mexican electronics firms. To get the goods,

> some vendors . . . travel to the U.S. border by car or truck, or meet airplanes at clandestine landing strips. . . . And despite crackdowns, much of the merchandise comes by way of the Mexico City airport. One vendor claims he has witnessed customs agents there using calculators to count their "tips" while smugglers loaded up a truckload of color-television sets.[58]

In the face of massive smuggling, the rigid Mexican ban on VCRs and videocassettes imposed in 1982 was altered somewhat in March 1985 to permit some machines and tapes to enter.[59]

Iran has a huge black market on which VCRs were sold in 1982 for the equivalent of $10,000.[60] Early on, the Khomeini government banned VCRs and many other luxuries, for economic reasons.[61] But smuggling and black marketeering — which hindered President Carter's efforts at a trade boycott during the hostage crisis — have rendered these imports bans quite ineffective.[62] By January 1985, the Iranian economy had become so precarious that all imports with the exception of food and arms were "unofficially halted,"[63] but it remains to be seen whether this will work any better than bans imposed previously.

In short, the world's black markets, where everything is illegal, provide the perfect conduit for VCRs to enter countries secretly and, just as secretly, to be transferred between private parties. It is ironic that this new, hitherto unheard-of access to information by the formerly deprived — an ideal so touted by the democracies — has no discernible relationship to a democratic game plan. As seen here, and as will be discussed in later chapters, it is largely a gift of global chaos and economic, legal, and political breakdown.

NOTES

[1]S. K. Ray, *Economics of the Black Market.* Westview Press, Boulder, CO 1981.

[2]Guenter Reimann, *The Black Market. Inevitable Child of Statism.* Pamphlet No. 35, Henry Regnery Co., Hindsdale, IL 1948.

[3]*Ibid,* p. 9.

[4]Josef Silverstein, "Burma. A Time for Decision," *Current History,* December 1984, p. 422.

[5]*Ibid.*

[6]*Ibid.*

[7]*Ibid.,* and also:

Amy Bermar, "Burma," *The Boston Sunday Globe,* November 4, 1984, p. 89.

Paisal Sricharatchanya, "The Real Market is Black," *Far Eastern Economic Review,* May 17, 1984, pp. 80, 82.

"Burma's Capitalist Road," *The Economist,* March 9, 1985, p. 75.

[8]Paisal Sricharatchanya, "The Real Market is Black," *Far Eastern Economic Review,* May 17, 1984, pp. 80, 82.

[9]Denis D. Gray, "Blue Jeans and 'E.T' Have Crept in but Burma Remains Isolated," *The Associated Press,* January 27, 1983, (NEXIS).

[10]Josef Silverstein, "Burma. A Time for Decision," *Current History,* December 1984, pp. 422ff.

Paisal Sricharatchanya, "The Real Market is Black," *Far Eastern Economic Review,* May 17, 1984, pp. 80, 82.

[11]S. K. Ray, *Economics of the Black Market.* Westview Press, Boulder, CO, 1981, pp. 47, 48.

See also:

Kamal Nayan Kabra, *The Black Economy In India.* Chanakya Publications, Delhi, 1982, for further information on India's total black economy.

Paul A. Gigot, "Halfway Across the Ganges," *The Wall Street Journal,* April 10, 1985, p. 28.

[12]Stuart Auerbach, "Smugglers Thrive in Protectionist India," *The Washington Post,* July 21, 1982, p. A-19.

[13]"Living Conveniently On The Left. A Thriving Network of Hidden Entrepreneurs," *Time,* June 23, 1980, p. 50.

See also:

Nicholas Daniloff, "It Takes Stealth and Bribery to Get By in Russia," *U.S. News & World Report,* November 9, 1981, pp. 41–42.

"Soap Opera. Shopping at the 'Black Hole,' " *Time,* April 27, 1981, p. 45.

Chryss Galassi with William E. Schmidt, "Starman's Scam and the Nochnik Bust," *Newsweek,* April 14, 1980, p. 48.

[14]Ned Temco, "Kremlin Sees Threat in Uncensored Videocassettes," *The Christian Science Monitor,* May 12, 1983, p. 2.

Among articles discussing black markets in VCRs and cassettes in the Soviet Union and Eastern Europe are:

Philip Taubman, "Oh Comrade, Can I Borrow Your Rambo Cassette?" *The New York Times,* December 9, 1985, p. A-2.

Philip Taubman, "Soviet Pans 'Rocky' and 'Rambo' Films," *The New York Times,* January 4, 1986, p. 3.

John Iams, "T-Shirts Symbolized Anti-Soviet Ideals," *United Press International,* August 26, 1984 (NEXIS).

Janusz Bugajski, "A Boom in Private Video Recorders," Situation Report, Poland/10, *Radio Free Europe Research,* Radio Free Europe-Radio Liberty, October 29, 1984, pp. 20–21.

Teresa Hanicka, "Underground Video Tape Production," Situation Report, Poland/8, *Radio Free Europe Research,* Radio Free Europe-Radio Liberty, May 21, 1985, pp. 23–24.

V. S., "On the Verge of the Video Revolution," Situation Report, Czechoslovakia/9, *Radio Free Europe Research,* Radio Free Europe-Radio Liberty, June 3, 1985, pp. 31–33.

George Jahn, "Video Cassette Black Market Flourishes in Hungary," *The Associated Press,* April 26, 1985 (NEXIS).

Steven Koppany, "Unprepared Regime Scrambles to Meet Challenges of the Video Era," Situation Report, Hungary/10, *Radio Free Europe Research,* Radio Free Europe-Radio Liberty, September 4, 1985, pp. 17–23.

G. S., "Video Wave Hits Bulgaria," Situation Report, Bulgaria/3, *Radio Free Europe Research,* Radio Free Europe-Radio Liberty, February 15, 1984, pp. 4–6.

[15]B. Jicinski, "The East Bloc's Market for Media Imports," *The Wall Street Journal,* September 19, 1984, p. 33.

[16]*Ibid.*

[17]*Ibid.*

[18]*Ibid.*

Another source has confirmed that most videotapes confiscated by Russian customs officials are not destroyed, and probably eventually make their way into the domestic market. The Soviet Union. Personal communications.

[19]Arthur Jones, "The Jaruzelski Index," *Forbes*, February 13, 1984, pp. 45–46.

[20]*Ibid.*, p. 45.

[21]*Ibid.*

[22]*Ibid.*, and also:

Jersrzy Pomorski, "Waiting for Video," *InterMedia*, July/September 1983, p. 66.

[23]Arthur Jones, "The Jaruzelski Index," *Forbes*, February 13, 1984, pp. 45–46.

[24]Douglas Stanglin. Personal communications.

[25]*Ibid.*

[26]*Ibid.*

[27]David Binder, "Yugoslavs Feel the Pinch of Economic Curbs," *The New York Times*, November 7, 1982, p. A-7.

[28]Alan Cowell, "Lagos, Oil Boom Fading, Scarred by Vast Growth," *The New York Times*, May 22, 1983, p. A-14.

[29]Scheherezade Faramarzi, "Lebanon Cracks Down on Smugglers," *The Associated Press*, April 7, 1983 (NEXIS).

[30]*Ibid.*

[31]*Ibid.*

[32]"Lebanon Threatens Illegal Ports," *The Boston Globe*, October 28, 1984, p. 1.

[33]Douglas Watson, "Syria's Assad Holds High Cards in the Mideast," *U.S. News & World Report*, February 13, 1984, p. 30.

[34]"Syrian Curb on Smuggling," *The Middle East*, September 1984, pp. 43–44.

[35]William Branigin, "Viets, Khmers Locked in Battle," *The Boston Globe*, December 31, 1984.

See also:

Mark Whitaker with Melinda Liu and Kim Willenson, "Cambodia's Agony: Hanoi Hits Again," *Newsweek*, January 7, 1985, pp. 10–21.

Paul Quinn-Judge, "Christmas Assault," *Far Eastern Economic Review*, pp. 32–33.

[36]Robert Kaylor, "As Troubles Mount for Communist Vietnam-," *U.S. News & World Report*, January 14, 1985, pp. 25–27.

[37]Robert Kaylor, "A Decade After Saigon's Fall, a Painful Peace," *U.S. News & World Report*, January 21, 1985, p. 45.

[38]*Ibid.*

[39]*Ibid.*

[40]Julia Leung, "Hong Kong's Boats Land Best Catches in the 'China Trade,' " *The Wall Street Journal*, January 16, 1981, pp. 1, 10. Reprinted in Burgess Laughlin, *Black Markets Around the World*, Loompanics Unlimited, Mason, MI, 1981, p. 69.

[41]"China Cracks Down on Smuggling by Organizations," *The Xinhua General Overseas News Service*, August 6, 1985 (NEXIS).

[42]*Ibid.*

[43]*Ibid.*

[44]"China. Beclouded by Greed," *The Economist*, August 10, 1985, p. 50.

[45]*Ibid.*

[46]Pico Iyer, "The Second Revolution. Deng's Reforms are Taking China on a Courageous if Uncharted Course," *Time*, September 23, 1985, pp. 52, 55.

[47]"Dateline: Beijing," *The Xinhua General Overseas News Service*, September 27, 1985 (NEXIS).

[48]*Ibid.*

[49]*Ibid.*

[50]Slobodan Stankovic, " 'Enigmatic Sources of Income' in Soviet Bloc Countries," RAD Background Report, Eastern Europe/288, *Radio Free Europe Research,* Radio Free Europe-Radio Liberty, December 30, 1983, p. 1.

[51]*Ibid.*

[52]*Ibid.,* pp. 2–3.

[53]*Ibid.,* p. 3.

For illegal uses of state property in the USSR, see the references listed under Note 13.

[54]"Cocaine Trade Comes to Bolivia City, Creating Wealth, Eroding Agriculture," *The Wall Street Journal,* March 25, 1981, p. 27. Reprinted as "Bolivian Cocaine Traders Raise Workers Wages," in Burgess Laughlin, *Black Markets Around the World,* Loompanics Unlimited, Mason, MI, 1981, pp. 74–75.

See also:

Roberto Junguito and Calor Caballero, "Illegal Trade Transactions and The Underground Economy of Columbia," in *The Underground Economy in The U.S. and Abroad,* Vito Tanzi, ed., Lexington Books, Lexington, MA 1982. This source includes a discussion of underground economies in many countries, including Israel, the USSR, Italy, and the U.S., in addition to Colombia.

Vito Tanzi, "The Underground Economy. The Causes and Consequences of This World-wide Phenomenon," *Finance and Development,* December 1983, pp. 10–13.

"Burma and Thailand. Battle of the Flowers," *The Economist,* March 9, 1985, p. 38.

Nicholas B. Tatro, "Egypt's Nile Valley Grows World's Best Opium," *The Oregonian,* December 26, 1978, p. A-6. Reprinted in Burgess Laughlin, *Black Markets Around The World,* Loompanics Unlimited, Mason, MI, 1981, pp. 41–43. This source says that in the 1970s, it was estimated that an Egyptian farmer, whose per capita income is usually only $250 a year, "could earn $35,000 an acre growing opium" (p. 42, Laughlin).

[55]Steve Frazier, "A Slum Black Market in Mexico Is a Part of The Establishment," *The Wall Street Journal,* March 25, 1985, p. 1.

[56]*Ibid.*

[57]*Ibid.*

[58]*Ibid.*

[59]"Odd Saga of Mexican Homevid. How it Came to Pass That VCRs and Videocassettes Became Smugglers Items," *Variety,* March 20, 1985, p. 96.

[60]Charles J. Hanley, "Today's Focus: In The Age of Khomeini, Tehran Moves at Half Step," *The Associated Press,* November 23, 1982 (NEXIS).

[61]Ray Vicker, "Dubai's Traders Are Building A Thriving Trade Smuggling Goods into Iran," *The Wall Street Journal,* May 7, 1980, p. 48. Reprinted as "Dubai's Enterprising Traders Smuggle Goods Into Iran," in Burgess Laughlin, *Black Markets Around the World,* Loompanics Unlimited, Mason, MI, 1981, p. 36.

[62]*Ibid.*

[63]Lelia Hemmat and Philip Marfleet, "Terhan's Great Debate," *The Middle East,* April 1985, p. 51.

CHAPTER FIVE

The Role of Migrants in VCR Penetration

Many sources mention that the first VCRs were introduced into their countries by migrants returning from work abroad. Among countries where migrants have played an early and/or important role in VCR penetration are Bangladesh, Bulgaria and most other Eastern European countries, Egypt, Guyana, India, Jamaica, the Philippines, Pakistan, Somalia, Turkey, and Yugoslavia.[1] China received many of its initial VCRs as gifts to relatives from returning overseas Chinese.[2]

Major sources of VCRs obtained by migrants have been the oil-rich Gulf states, where the needs for massive migrant labor almost coincided with the emergence of VCRs in the 1970s. VCRs have similarly been obtained by migrants to Western Europe, which "called in an army of millions of migrants"[3] during the 1960s. In 1980, there were still more than 6 million legal migrants in Western Europe and a goodly number more of illegals.[4]*

Many of the poorer nations have come to rely heavily on migrant remittances as a source of income and foreign exchange. A 1981 World Bank report compared 1978–79 percentages of remittances to percentages of merchandise exports of some labor-exporting countries. It found that remittances comprised 42.5% of that for merchandise exports for Yugoslavia, 76.7% for Turkey, 68.9% for Portugal, 51.3% for Morocco, 88.0% for Egypt, 76.5% for Pakistan, 59.6% for Upper Volta, and 33.0% for Mali. Remittances were "practically the only source of foreign exchange earnings . . . for the Yemen People's Democratic Republic, the Yemen Arab Republic and Jordan during this period," the report said.[6]

Both the numbers of migrants and the importance of their remittances to their countries have soared since that time.[7] In early 1984, there were a reported 2 to 3 million Asian laborers in the Middle East. Pakistan had 700,000 workers in the Gulf area, remitting 9% of that country's GNP and financing 86% of its foreign deficit. South Korea had 150,000 workers, remitting 3% to 4% of its GNP, and the Philippines had 340,000 migrants, remitting 3% to 4% of its GNP.[8]

---

* Illegal migrants are to be found all over Europe. There are an estimated 20,000 Portuguese, 2000 African, and more than 1000 Asian illegals just in Geneva. Illegal immigrants from Egypt, Somalia, Ethiopia, Ghana, India, Pakistan, the Philippines, and Indonesia are now presenting a problem in Italy, Greece, Spain, and Portugal. Because of heavy tourism in these countries, it is practically impossible to tighten borders.[5]

A report in fall 1984, based on World Bank figures, showed remittances providing nearly as much foreign exchange as exports for Pakistan and Upper Volta. They amounted to more than 60% for Egypt, Turkey, and Portugal, and nearly 40% for Bangladesh and Yugoslavia.[9] Jordan's remittances grew from not quite $7.5 million in 1972 to more than $408 million in 1981.[10]

Remittances are the great attraction of foreign work for both the migrant and his government, "but priorities of government and families do not necessarily coincide. . . ."[11] If they had their way, governments would have migrants remit a high percentage of their wages, preferably through some sort of controllable banking system. The Philippines and South Korea attempt to enforce a 70% remittance of the migrant's earnings. The migrant has other ideas, however. It is no fun to leave his village and family (most migrants are young men and married) and go to work in a strange country. However, there is the lure of making five to ten times the money that can be made at home (when there are jobs), of furnishing families with consumer and even luxury and status items, and of purchasing something of value which can later be vended, more than likely on the black market.

If the involved government wants to get migrants to go abroad to work, and to remit at least some significant portion of their wages, it must be willing to make compromises. Turkey, for instance, reduces compulsory military service in return for remittance of a "specified amount in foreign exchange. . . ."[12] Turkish building contractors in the Middle East increased from 22 in 1978 to 283 in 1983.[13] There are 120,000 Turkish workers there, remitting $500 million a year. This is in addition to the 773,000 Turks at work in Western Europe.[14]

Some countries (including the Sudan) pay black market interest rates on migrant bank deposits as an incentive for remitting through official channels.[15] But part of the compromise is most often that the migrant is allowed to bring in much-wanted merchandise and consumer items.[16] Governments practice such leniency, not because they want to, but because, otherwise, both the money and the merchandise will simply enter the black market. One source says:

> Any attempt at more official control on the part of the labor-exporting state tends to increase the number of informal transfers . . . efforts to raise more central revenue out of migration for employment by imposing import taxes brings about an increase in the clandestine transit of migrant workers and illegal imports. . . .[17]

Money or merchandise may be "either carried by the migrants themselves or handled by agents who specialized in black market transfers. . . ."[18] Omanis, for instance, and it may be assumed, other migrants, use relatives, trusted agents, and friends who travel (both legally and illegally) between the countries of employment and origin to transfer the remittances, both in cash and as goods.[19]

In 1984, the 2 to 3 million Egyptian migrants officially remitted $3.4 billion. The actual figure is thought to be from $6 to $10 billion.[20]

The numbers of migrants involved in consumer goods transfers may be much higher than the migrants abroad at any one given time. Turnover of migrant labor is high, especially in countries like Saudi Arabia, where workers are not allowed to bring their families and the period they stay is limited. Many migrants are illegals and go uncounted. (Although official numbers are much lower, between 2 and 4 million Pakistanis may have worked in the Gulf area from 1971 onward.)[21] Those who remain migrants often return home and then go out again. Thus, the potential technological couriers for VCRs and other consumer items number in the many millions.

Migrants who introduce VCRs are important in more ways than numbers. While some are professionals and highly skilled individuals from cities, vast numbers come from the ranks of the poorest villagers. Thus, VCRs reach the less affluent, not just the elites, as is often the case where VCRs are brought in by other types of travelers.* Having been exposed to new ideas and to more money than they have ever had before, migrant workers are frequently reluctant to return to their old village life style. They may become disaffected and/or migrate to the city, creating social and political difficulties. Those people who have not migrated are jealous of the increased status of the migrant — represented by VCRs or other ostentatious consumer products. The migrant may also provide his family with added income by using his VCR to give (often clandestine) shows for admission, if only a few pennies.[22]

Pakistan is an example of the complex interplay between the migrant, his VCR, and his government. Even as returned migrants use VCRs to escape from Pakistan's fundamentalist Islamic television programming, President Zia is pushing for more fundamentalism. He is also pushing for wide "open door" migration in order to gain "preferred status as a recipient of Official Development Assistance (ODA) from the oil-rich MENA countries . . . "[23] To the Pakistanis, as to other developing country migrants, "the video-cassette recorder and other electronic gadgetry have become necessities rather than luxuries. . . ."[24] That is, they are becoming "necessities" as status symbols in the villages, where

the saying *Dubai Chalo* — "let us go to Dubai" — which is the equivalent of the expression "Westward ho" in Western tradition — has become part of Pakistani

---

* The migrant may, and often does, sell his VCR on the black market for great profit, and in this way it may reach the affluent.

culture . . . signif[ying] the possibility of gathering [wealth] relatively quick[ly]. . . .[25]

"Dubai Chalo" and "Visa Dubai da" (Visa for Dubai) are two Pakistani films in Urdu and Punjabi.[26] Susannah Tarbush describes this Pakistani desire to show that they can gain riches and status:

> Forty miles south of Islamabad lies a village of some 300 people, which has no electricity or running water and is accessible only by a dirt road. In the middle of the cluster of baked-mud houses is a gleaming new concrete and brick room in one corner of which is stacked a 22-inch television set, an unpacked videocassette recorder and a stereo tape-recorder.
>
> The room is the home of an agricultural laborer working on an Abu Dhabi vegetable farm. "We are waiting for the government to put in electricity, but even without it we feel rich with all these goods around us," says his wife.[27]

The importance of VCRs as status symbols has been mentioned for many developing countries, for the major communist countries, and also for the democracies.

Until recently in Yugoslavia, *only* migrant workers were allowed to bring in VCRs legally, since an import restriction on TVs was applied to VCRs (and to computers). The cost of a VCR also exceeded an import ceiling.[28]* Yugoslavia was thought in 1984 to have about 350,000 videocassette recorders.[29] Yugoslav families who go out to visit people in other countries have routinely smuggled VCRs in,[30] but travel has been limited for economic reasons. Yugoslavia is heavily dependent on remittances, receiving $2 billion a year — the same amount as it receives from tourism — from some 700,000 to 1 million migrant workers.

While no Eastern European nation** approaches Yugoslavia's scale of migrant labor, Romania and Bulgaria, for instance, each have substantial numbers of migrants in the Gulf countries. The Bulgarians have between 20,000 and 50,000 migrant workers building parts of airfields and large apartment buildings. Wherever the contractor is a state enterprise, there are migrant workers from all Eastern European countries. The state enterprise pays for the migrant's travel and controls part of his pay by depositing it for him. But the same thing holds for Eastern European migrants as for those of other labor-furnishing countries: If the government doesn't give them some "perks," such as bringing in consumer goods, then they won't go abroad and work.[31]

---

* New legislation due in 1985 was expected to remove both of these restrictions.

** Because it is a socialist country, Yugoslavian data is often lumped with that of Eastern Europe. But its restrictions are mild and in no way compare with those of the Soviet bloc countries.

Other types of Eastern European migrants are people who have lived a long time in some Western country, but who retire in their homelands because they can live there so much more cheaply. When they return, they take along consumer goods, including VCRs, with their other personal belongings. Many Poles, for instance, come to the United States to visit relatives living here. The relatives get them illegal jobs and they overstay, sometimes as much as 10 years. The exact scale of this is not known, but it is in "the tens of thousands," and could be as much as 50,000 to 100,000.[32] The Poles are the biggest group of this type, but there are also similar groups of other Eastern Europeans. When they do return to their homelands, they take along desirable consumer goods, with VCRs undoubtedly among them.

In addition to Bulgarian nationals who migrate, Turkish migrants to Western Europe travel through Bulgaria enroute home to Turkey. They often take home a new car loaded with consumer goods, including videocassette recorders. On the railroads, too, the workers bring along huge cartons of such equipment. They get past the border with this material, although "there are undoubtedly payments for the privilege." Some of these items are presumed to be sold, somewhere along the way, in Bulgaria.[33]

There are many other migrants all over the world. South Africa has lots of guest labor; Nigeria used to. Although little information has specifically emerged on this, the U.S. and Canada are undoubtedly sources of VCRs for migrants from Mexico and the Caribbean.

NOTES

[1]Bangladesh. Personal communications. See also Fred Arnold, "Asian Migrants Pump Oil Money Into Homelands," *The Wall Street Journal,* March 5, 1984, p. 31, for the migrant situation in Bangladesh and other nations.

Eastern Europe. Personal communications. See also G. S. "Bulgaria Goes Into the Video Business," Situation Report, Bulgaria/13, *Radio Free Europe Research,* Radio Free Europe-Radio Liberty, October 10, 1984, for the overall Bulgarian VCR situation.

Yehai Aboubakr, "Egypt. Late Arrivals," *InterMedia,* July/September, 1983, p. 48 for Egypt. See also Dennis Mullin, "Behind Egypt's Return to Favor in Arab World," *U.S. News & World Report,* November 12, 1984, pp. 41–42; Eric Rouleau, "Egypt's Identity Crisis. Struggling to Surmount Economic Ills and Islamic Extremism," *World Press Review,* November 1984, pp. 26–28; and H. D. S. Greenway, "Prosperity Grows Amid Crisis Chaos," *The Boston Globe,* March 10, 1985, p. 18, for Egypt's migrant situation.

Victor L. C. Forsythe, "Guyana. Video Parties-And Fewer Cars Stolen," *InterMedia,* July/September, 1983, pp. 52–53, for Guyana.

Tess Thomas, "Jamaica. The Miami Connection," *InterMedia,* July/September, 1983, p. 57, for Jamaica.

Nora C. Quebral, *The Video Recorder in Developing Countries,* speech, International Institute of Communications 1984 Annual Conference, Berlin, September 22, 1984, for the Philippines.

Javed Jabbar, "Pakistan. A Cautious Welcome," *InterMedia,* July/September 1983, pp. 65–66. See also "Slump in Pakistan's Remittances," *The Middle East,* January 1985, p. 21, among others, for Pakistan's remittances.

Somalia. Personal communications.

Turkey and Eastern Europe. Personal communications. See also Emel Anil, "Bootleg Movies are Big Business in Turkey," *The Associated Press*, February 28, 1984 (NEXIS).

For Yugoslavia, personal communications, Yugoslavia and Eastern Europe.

[2]Orville Schell, *To Get Rich is Glorious. China in the 80's.* Pantheon Books, New York, 1984, pp. 179–180.

See also:

Ian Burma, "Call of the Motherland. China Uses Patriotism to Encourage the Support of its Overseas Sons," *Far Eastern Economic Review*, November 22, 1984, pp. 46–48; and Li Bo, "China. Gifts From Overseas," *InterMedia*, July/September, 1983, p. 44.

[3]David R. Francis, "West Europe's Guest Workers. Living Conditions have Improved, but Discrimination Persists." *The Christian Science Monitor*, January 25, 1985, pp. 9–10.

[4]*Ibid.*

[5]*Ibid.*

[6]Gurushi Swamy, *International Migrant Workers' Remittances: Issues and Prospects*, World Bank Staff Working Paper No, 481, August 1981, p. 7–10.

[7]Fred Arnold, "Asian Migrants Pump Oil Money Into Homelands," *The Wall Street Journal*, March 5, 1984, p. 31.

[8]*Ibid.*

[9]Shahid Javed Burki, "International Migration: Implications for Labor Exporting Countries," *The Middle East Journal*, Volume 38, No. 4, Autumn, 1984, p. 672.

[10]Charles B. Keely and Bassam Saket, "Jordanian Migrant Workers in the Arab Region: A Case Study of Consequences for Labor Supplying Countries," *The Middle East Journal*, Volume 38, No. 4, Autumn, 1984, p. 687.

[11]*Ibid.*, p. 688.

[12]"Remittances: The Most Tangible Reward," in Ismail Serageldin, James A. Socknat, Stace Birks, Bob Li, and Clive A. Sinclair, *Manpower and International Labor Migration in the Middle East and North Africa*, Oxford University Press, for the World Bank, 1983, p. 90.

[13]Jeff Trimble, "Turkey Bounces Back from the Brink," *U.S. News & World Report*, April 1, 1985, p. 42.

[14]David R. Francis, "West Europe's Guest Workers," *The Christian Science Monitor*, January 25, 1985, pp. 9–10.

[15]"Remittances: The Most Tangible Reward," in Ismail Serageldin et al., *Manpower and International Labor Migration in the Middle East and North Africa.* Oxford University Press, for the World Bank, 1983, p. 91.

[16]*Ibid.*, pp. 90–91.

[17]*Ibid.*, p. 90.

[18]*Ibid.*, p. 89.

[19]*Ibid.*

[20]H. D. S. Greenway, "Prosperity Grows Amid Cairo's Chaos," *The Boston Globe*, March 10, 1985, p. 18.

[21]Shahid Javed Burki, "International Migration: Implications for Labor Exporting Countries," *The Middle East Journal*, Volume 38, No. 4, Autumn, 1984, p. 677.

[22]Fred Arnold, "Asian Migrants Pump Oil Money Into Homelands," *The Wall Street Journal*, March 5, 1984, p. 31, among others.

Javed Jabbar, "Pakistan. A Cautious Welcome," *InterMedia*, July/September 1983, p. 66.

[23]Robert LaPorte, Jr., "The Ability of South and East Asia to Meet the Labor Demands of the Middle East and North Africa," *The Middle East Journal*, Volume 38, No. 4, Autumn 1984, p. 708.

[24]Susannah Tarbush, "The New Nomads. Manpower in the Gulf. The Labor Exporters. Pakistan," *The Middle East*, February 1983, p. 30.

[25]Akbar S. Ahmed, " 'Dubai Chalo', Problems in the Ethnic Encounter Between Middle Eastern and South Asian Muslim Societies," *Asian Affairs,* Volume XV, Pt. III, October 1984, p. 263.

[26]*Ibid.*

[27]Susannah Tarbush, "The New Nomads. Manpower in the Gulf. The Labor Exporters. Pakistan," *The Middle East,* February 1983, p. 30.

[28]Yugoslavia. Personal communications.

[29]*Ibid.*

[30]Eastern Europe. Personal communications. Douglas Stanglin mentioned the many Polish migrants who earn dollars abroad as a reason why the Polish government tolerates the possession of dollars. Douglas Stanglin. Personal communications.

[31]Eastern Europe. Personal communications.

[32]*Ibid.*

[33]*Ibid.*

CHAPTER SIX

The Software: Videocassette Distribution, Including the Role of Organized Crime

The introduction of videocassettes has followed an almost uncanny pattern of uniformity worldwide.[1] In the very beginning, a few cassettes were introduced by individual travelers, migrants, privileged elites, tourists, petty smugglers, and others. Clubs were soon formed by groups of a few people, for cassette swapping and to get a little money up front to buy more titles. In most countries, these clubs were overtaken very quickly by hordes of video outlets which dealt in illegal as well as legal tapes, and themselves often turned out copy after copy. The clubs then either went out of business or else converted themselves to the same types of activities. Certain aspects of this uniformity can be seen even in the most restricted countries.

There were brief efforts globally to sell videocassettes, but, in most cases, this proved to be too costly for patrons. Within just months, rental became the rule, giving mass distribution to all comers. Price cutting ensued, so that video rentals dropped from a beginning price of the equivalent generally of about $5 to about $1 or even as low as 50 cents for overnight, or a weekend.

The uniformity and efficiency of this global distribution is all the more remarkable since, in the beginning, the big Hollywood movie types refused to distribute programming. Those who got in on the ground floor were some small independent companies and the pirates.[2]* Some of this may be credited to widescale global communications — everybody just followed everybody else's example. But it also seems logical to conjecture that, with a suddenly popular product, and in the absence of some large legal group in control, some or several well-organized illegal groups got their hands on the ropes of videocassette distribution very early.

Everything that can be said for the penetration of VCR hardware is true — in spades — for videocassette programming. Wherever VCRs go, videocassettes follow. Videocassettes of every sort have swiftly penetrated globally, they are often introduced by migrants and other travelers, and they avail themselves of the world's black markets for distribution. They have, in

---

* The word "pirate" is rather indiscriminately applied both to the person or group illegally reproducing and distributing cassettes in violation of copyright, and to those who actually smuggle cassettes across borders. "Pirated" should be reserved for cassettes in copyright violation.

addition, the attributes of being small enough to be easily smuggled, of being readily reproducible either before or after smuggling, and of being, more often than not, pirated.

Through a change in labeling, or a substitution of a small portion of the tape beginning, "undesirable" material can easily pass a customs system as something innocuous. Political tapes went into the Philippines under the guise of pornography[3] (see Chapter 9), and porno pours into Canada from the U.S. labeled as comedy and other materials. Canada's Revenue Minister Pierre Bussieres has said that "clever methods to disguise the cassettes are used to slip them by inspectors . . . " and that "foreign exporters often change the film titles to make them seem harmless and make it next to impossible to catch at the border."[4] In Pakistan, video outlets are said to

acquire — invariably pirated — master versions of new Indian movies released in Bombay just two or three days earlier with remarkable speed, via the smugglers' Dubai connection.[5]

Indian movies have been banned in Pakistan since 1956. *The Associated Press* says, for Turkey,

theoretically . . . video cassettes must . . . pass through the censor to enter the country. But the cassettes are so small, so easy to declare untaped and so abundant that effective official control has so far proven impossible.[6]

Like a number of countries which are updating their legislation to take videocassettes into account, Turkey put through a copyright law which became effective in November 1983, "call[ing] for prison terms ranging from one month to three years for copyright violations, and all video cassettes must have special markings to show that the distributor has the copyright."[7] However, as one Turkish official put it, " 'Turks are expert at getting around official regulations. As long as there is a high demand and good profits to be made, tapes will keep coming, with or without copyright.' "[8]

In Russia, the Black Sea agricultural area of Krasnodarsky krai is a big area not only for health spas but also for smuggling. In Novorossiysk, south of Krasnodar

smuggling is "a big problem" in the seaport used by thousands of sailors from all corners of the world . . . more than 25 percent of those dealing in illegal goods were [said to be] foreigners. A large amount of the traffic involves scarce or unavailable Western goods such as blue jeans, T-shirts, records, tapes and video tapes that command high prices on the black market.[9]

In addition to smuggled tapes, Tallinn,* in Estonia, where Finnish television can be received, has become "the unofficial video recording headquarters of the USSR."[10] Here,

> the best of Finnish (which can also mean American, British, Italian, German, or Brazilian) television is recorded in apartments where reception is best. Sometimes Russian-language voice-overs are added. The cassettes are distributed to Moscow, Lenigrad, and other cities with no fear of border controls for those who carry them on Aeroflot planes. . . .[11]

Such videotapes include American political debates and news of other political events, including those taking place inside Russia.

Reports of the availability of videocassettes in Russia vary. *The New York Times,* in December 1985, said

> in many ways, the video business remains a primitive and costly one compared with the business in the West. The going rate for having a movie dubbed into Russian is about 30 rubles. A ruble is $1.28 at the official exchange rate. . . .[12]

Dubbing is nevertheless replacing the person hired for the occasion to translate while the movie is going on. Blank tapes are selling for the equivalent of $60 to $70, and western movies for the equivalent of $250 to $320, on the Soviet black market.[13]

But, despite the expense, videocassettes are spreading. Actor Mel Ferrer, in Russia in spring 1985 to appear in the NBC miniseries "Peter the Great," is reported to have said, " 'videocassettes are all the rage in the youth underground . . . you can get a film two weeks after its opening in the United States. . . .' "[14] Indications are that cassettes, while still limited even as compared to those in Eastern European countries, are becoming more and more readily available.[15] Illegal films are sufficiently disturbing to the Soviet government that it has opened its own videocassette rental outlets for approved films. *The New York Times* says

> the first video rental store, called a Videoteka, opened in May [1985] in Voronezh. . . . Since then other outlets have opened around the Soviet Union. . . . There are two rental outlets in Moscow. One is in the basement of a movie theater near the farmer's market. . . . The store has a library of 270 films . . . The movies, all of which were made in the Soviet Union or the Soviet bloc, with the exception of a few made in India, range from historical epics such as Sergei Eisenstein's "Ivan the Terrible" to current comedies and children's films.[16]

---

* Tallinn is a "center for dissidents opposed to the Russification of Estonia," according to Donald Shanor.

The cost to rent these approved cassettes is not cheap but quite reasonable, rental for a day costing 2 or 3 rubles.

In the new town part of Warsaw in 1984, at least one legal private dealer was quietly but openly renting "a roomful" of videocassettes, along with his record and music business.[17] His tapes, all pirated, were obtained from "friends" in West Berlin and London, and probably the United States. This dealer, who stocked popular cassettes such as "Caligula" and "Last Tango in Paris", etc., was very proud to have obtained a cassette of "The Day After" before it was shown on British television. He claimed to be cutting into the Warsaw cinema business by distributing films such as "Tootsie" months before the theaters could get them. To prevent others from pirating his pirated tapes, he made a point of retaping them to the edge of fuzziness before rental. He handled the hard currency problem by paying zlotys for the support of the relatives in Poland of the Westerners who provided the cassettes to him. Cassettes rented for the equivalent of $6 or $7 a night, but, for the more affluent, this was very affordable with the zloty. Variations in broadcast standards must be overcome by some commercial means, but this dealer seemed to have mastered the problem. To get past the language barrier in Poland, as was done in Russia, one person will often read all the parts in Polish. This is often put on an audiotape, to be played back with the videocassette.[18] Hard core pornographic videocassettes are handled by a few people in the Polish black market. They are not as widespread as other types of videocassettes, according to this source.[19] It should be noted that there is no censorship of unofficially available videocassettes in Poland,[20] nor does there appear to be in any of the other Eastern bloc countries. The Poles have now moved into their own underground production of politically oriented or forbidden videocassette programming (see Chapter 7).

In Czechoslovakia, a source observed,

> videotapes of Western films, both standard fare and pornography, are widely circulated, copied illegally, and even rented — all outside the regular channels of state control.[21]

The Czechs are also attempting to produce or control their own programming in a thus far vain effort to blunt the influence of foreign products[22] (See Chapter 10.)

In Hungary, dealers in black market videocassettes are said to earn up to "70,000 forints ($1,400) a month, or 14 times the average wage."[23] Here, black marketeers even pirate the tapes officially made available in tape rental libraries by the Hungarian government. Radio Budapest is credited with reporting

> "Make your selection, pay for it, rent it, play it, in other words, use it and then return it. These are the principles according to which every rental shop in the

world operates. Except in our country. Here the kind customer not only views the rented film thoroughly but he also copies it. Then he takes the rented cassette apart, removes the original tape, replaces it with the copy, reassembles his own and the rented cassettes, leaves the original, better quality version at home in the cabinet, and returns the poor quality copy to the shelves of MOKEP's video library."[24]

Hungary, like several of the Eastern European countries, is attempting to develop a program aimed at controlling VCRs and cassettes (see Chapter 10), but its announced intentions for video uses—"party propaganda, public and higher education, entertainment and propaganda directed abroad. . . ."[25] are not likely to lower the appeal of the black market.

South of the United States, video piracy is simple "because U.S. satellite signals are easily picked up in the Caribbean, Central America and Northern South America. . . ."[26] The feature films on Ted Turner's satellite television are pirated for cable and play 24 hours a day in Panama.[27]* Videocassette piracy is rampant in Panama, with one duplication plant keeping 100 copying machines continuously running. Panama is said to export from 20,000 to 30,000 pirated videocassettes a month to Latin American countries, "especially to Colombia, Ecuador, and Mexico. . . ."[29] The chief producer of pirated cassettes in Panama is alleged to be Isaac Zafrani, who

drives a gold-colored Cadillac, and claims to have made "maybe $10 million" from an unlicensed videocassette empire that includes three duplicating plants, and a chain of clean, well-lit shops — among them the lucrative airport concession.[30]

When Warner Brothers, to feel out the Mexican videocassette market in 1984, released a test cassette of "The Jane Fonda Workout Tape," a pirated copy immediately appeared in competition. The pirated version, sold in major department stores, had a 1974 copyright label, although the tape wasn't made until nine years later. Pirated cassettes are also being sold at Tepito and Peritrece, the newest of Mexico City's major black market outlets. Tepito is said to have a list "of over 1000 titles" which are marketed openly. These videocassettes are mostly smuggled in from the U.S. and then copied. There is a six-month to year wait for American films in Mexico after they are released in the U.S. and Canada.[31]

Small legitimate videocassette markets have recently been set

---

* Blank tapes, also globally smuggled, make it easy to record intercepted satellite signals. For instance, when South Africa was denied both participation in the 1984 Los Angeles Olympics and a live transmission, signals were intercepted illegally to watch Zola Budd run. Videocassettes of the event, probably from outside and from illegal signal interception, were also quickly supplied to rental customers.[28]

up in Venezuela, Argentina, and Brazil, with others due in Mexico and Colombia. Most Latin American videocassettes are still pirated, however, with "tapes . . . being washed in Cuba . . . [and] purveyors . . . play[ing] [sic] a lively bootlegging trade on the coasts of Colombia and Peru. . . ."[32] All cassettes in Bolivia and Paraguay are said to be pirated.

Prerecorded tapes are often passed off as blanks. In fall 1984, the International Federation of Phonogram and Videogram Producers (IFPI) announced the seizure of 190,000 pirated videocassettes in Benin, Africa, which were on their way from Singapore to Benin's neighbor, Nigeria.[33] They had been declared as blank tapes, not only to conceal their pirated nature, but to escape the much higher prerecorded cassette customs duty. They were hardly blank, however, and included "tapes by Michael Jackson, Bob Marley, Dolly Parton, Marvin Gaye, Boney M and ABBA."[34]*

Although smuggled VCRs are often found wherever drugs, arms, etc. are being smuggled — the Khyber Pass and the Golden Crescent and Golden Triangle, for instance[43] — they have not been seen as specifically tied to organized crime. There is, however, substantial evidence that at least some portion of videocassette production and distribution has become an organ-

---

* IFPI is the London-based organization that acts as watchdog for the international record business, linking music and videotape business in 68 countries.[35] It is part of another international anti-piracy group formed in early 1984, the Joint Anti-Piracy Intelligence Group (JAPIG). Also involved in the Benin seizure were the International Maritime Bureau, the French composers group SACEM, the International Society of Composers, CISAC, and the Nigerian representative of the U.S.-based Black Music Association.[36] This is indicative of the cooperation that is being exerted to fight piracy. In 1982, the Motion Picture Association of America (MPAA), which itself has a worldwide chain of anti-piracy security offices, helped set up FACT (the Federation Against Copyright Theft) in London. " . . . Britain's PAL (Phase Alternation Line) television system is common to more than 50 countries . . . [says Jack Valenti] so films and programs can be taped for sales abroad."[37] Piracy in Britain was said to account for 70 to 80% of cassettes in 1982, but to have fallen to 60% in summer 1983 and 20% by early 1985 as a result of copyright law changes and efforts of controlling bodies.[38] These "controlled" figures must be taken with caution, for several reasons. Nobody knows just how much piracy there was, or now is, and, once "controlled," piracy tends to pop up elsewhere. Controllers may have been overly pessimistic about early figures and overly optimistic about later ones. It is known that piracy in Great Britain early on was extensive. "E.T." was premiered in London on December 9, 1982, but masses of British had been seeing it on videocassette since August. In late 1982, Norman Abbott, general secretary for British Videogram Association, said that, " 'Of the 6.7 million prerecorded cassettes currently circulating in the UK, 5.2 million are illegal copies.' "[39] In the Middle East, and East, and Southeast Asia, piracy remains rampant, and Singapore has emerged as a major new piracy center. Singapore seeks to strictly control videocassettes among its own people, requiring a censorship stamp on each one, but piracy is said to be 98% there.[40] Belgium has been a major center for French language and other Northern European cassette piracy.[41] In Scotland, where FACT has quite successfully controlled rental outlets, pirates simply set up mobile operations in factories and offices, operating well with no fixed base.[42]

ized crime function. Already in 1981, video pirates were making such in-roads that the representatives of various governments met in Geneva to try to determine how to combat them. *Reuters* reported,

> today's pirates have little of the glamour of their predecessors although the tak-ings are richer. Instead of operating on the high seas in leaky galleons, they work from back alleys with high-speed duplicators and a batch of cheap tapes.[44]

It quotes IFPI as saying,

> "nowadays, record pirates are often the same people who are active in other il-legal enterprises such as the trade in dangerous drugs" . . . [45]

The same source says it is clear that there are close links between organized crime and record piracy in the U.S. and Europe, and that "there are many indications of similar connections" in Southeast Asia. At the time of the above meeting, the World Intellectual Property Organization (WIPO) rep-resentative said, " 'We are not talking about the person at home who puts a record on cassette or who videotapes a television program. . . . We are talk-ing about big business. . . .' "[46] In December 1984, William Nix, director of antipiracy for the MPAA, made the same sort of statement:

> "We're not just fighting some video shop owner in Juarez that knocks off extra copies of 'Gremlins' for its customers. . . . We're being ripped off by pirates with millions of dollars in machine capital and international distribution net-works that work overnight."[47]

In 1982, *The Associated Press* reported:

> In the last five years, the illegal taping of movies and television has grown from a home hobby to a lucrative underground industry largely controlled, investi-gators say, by organized crime.

> The pirate godfathers include the Mafia, which provides master tapes and original prints of new movies for illegal copying even before they have gone on general release. . . .[48]

A 1976 U.S. Justice Department Task Force report on organized crime (which predates the videocassette business) traced the evolution of the entry until that time of U.S. organized crime groups into the area of pornography:

> Just when organized crime became involved in pornography is uncertain, but a contributing factor may have been a Supreme Court decision in 1967, *Redrup*

vs New York. This ruling left unclear what exactly constitutes pornography, thus making it difficult for law enforcement officers to make cases, but also making it hard for legitimate businesses to know if they were handling legal or illegal material. Thus legitimate distributors were unwilling to handle potentially pornographic material.

That development created a situation ripe for organized crime. . . .[49]

The *Report* describes how the New York Colombo crime "family" got control of the peep shows and the actual projection machines and pornographic films of New York City's Time Square area in the late 1960s. The Bonano family, it says, was involved in financing, producing, and distributing films, and had its own theaters, operating through many legitimate fronts on both coasts of the United States. The Colombo family, it says, "is said to have" put up the money for "Deep Throat," a pornographic best seller, while also distributing, for instance, legitimate Andy Warhol films.[50] The *Report* also notes,

> piracy is a big part of organized crime's pornography business. If a producer refuses to allow organized crime figures to distribute a film, those figures threaten piracy, among other actions. If its request is still refused, organized crime elements make their own copies of the film and distribute them widely, very often closing substantial markets to the legitimate producer.[51]

Chicago's Local 110 Moving Pictures Machine Operators Union was founded in 1915 by "labor racketeer Thomas Maloy," and has had a long and bloody history of control by Chicago mobsters.[52] George Browne and Willy Bioff, who controlled the local after Maloy was shot in the 1930s, went to jail for "extortion of millions of dollars from the heads of Hollywood's film studios. . . ."[53] This was a crime for which Al Capone's successor, Frank Nitti, was also indicted. There is said to be "no solid evidence" that the local is still controlled by mobsters, but "in 1980, the *Chicago Tribune* reported that federal investigators had 'identified 24 men with mob ties as members. . . .' "[54] These included " 'two sons and a brother of Anthony J. Accardo . . . the undisputed boss of the Chicago crime syndicate.' "[55]

Thus, it can be seen that the stage was well set for organized crime to get into the videocassette business. By 1980, crime groups had entered not only the pornographic videocassette business, but the business of illegal videocassettes in general.[56] In that year, a big crime bust was conducted in New York and other U.S. cities, during which members of the Bonano, Colombo, and Cavalcante (of New Jersey) "families" were arrested. The Cavalcante group runs Star Distributors, "one of the country's major porno suppliers."[57] During these raids, however, masters and video copies of a number of non-pornographic films, including "Kramer vs. Kramer," "The Deer Hunter," "A Clockwork Orange," and others, were confiscated.[58]

In February 1985, when a number of heads of American crime "families" were arrested, involvement in pirated audio- and video-cassettes were stated as being among their activities.[59] Those arrested were heads of the Gambino, Lucchese, Genovese, Colombo, and Bonano families.[60] The Bonano family was specifically said to have "recently moved into the production of hard-core pornography movies for use in home video recorders."[61] And the Colombo family was said to have "bought a facility to produce television movies."[62]

U.S. prosecutors who are moving to counter the spread of pornography by videocassette domestically say

> studies by law-enforcement agencies had repeatedly indicated that the production and distribution of pornographic films in America was largely controlled by organized crime.[63]

The efforts of prosecutors are now being directed, not at

> "adult" bookstores and "peepshow" establishments that have sold such videocassettes in the past, usually in downtown urban neighborhoods. Instead, they aim at the growing number of rental shops around the nation in middle-class neighborhoods, suburban shopping malls and other places previously off limits to "adult" businesses.[64]

The New York Times quotes Jane Miller of the Minneapolis Pornography Research Center as saying,

> "pornography is creeping into the mainstream" through videocassette records. . . . "What would have been off limits even in a red-light district a few years ago is now available for people to see in their living room". . . .[65]

Japan's Yakuza is said to be involved, at the very least, in procuring and distributing pornographic videotapes.[66]

In West Germany, Manfred Goeller, the general manager for the Association of Film Distributors, says that, in the business of "borrowing" hit film reels to make illegal videocassettes, there used to be

> many small-time operators concentrating on getting prints from firstrun houses, [but] the pirating now is concentrated in eight groups of Germans, some with links to the Mafia, but most linked to the German underworld.[67]

Variety reports:

> In one recent incident, police in Karlsruhe seized 4,450 videocassettes and 19 recorders belonging to a gang of Italians with Mafia connections who were seeking to control the illegal videocassettes sold to the more than 1,000,000 Italian workers and their families in this country [West Germany].[68]

Amid growing concern that the international pirates of videocassettes and records have linked up with organized crime in many countries, the IFPI sponsored a meeting of investigators from Austria, Germany, Holland, Spain, Switzerland, the UK., and the U.S. in October 1984.[69]

In 1982, an article concerning child pornography said that pornography, including films, was often created in the U.S. but then sent overseas for mass production and distribution.[70] Interestingly, these materials are often re-imported into the U.S. (mostly from Scandinavia). A similar phenomenon concerning non-pornographic films and dramas occurs in Egypt. There "programmes originally made in Egypt and reproduced abroad are smuggled back into the country to avoid copyright and other dues. . . ."[71] It would be interesting to know whether the same sort of thing, on a scale far beyond porno, is happening in the U.S., and probably elsewhere.

Pirating and smuggling of videocassettes is part of yet another recently stepped-up worldwide phenomenon — the production and global distribution of all manner of faked goods. These range from flashlight batteries to floppy discs; from toys to watches; from Charlie perfume, Revlon cosmetics, Jordache, Calvin Klein, and Levi Strauss jeans to Apple computers, computer software, and microchips; and from there to airplane, missile, and auto components.[72] The centers for these pirating operations are said to be in Brazil, and in Hong Kong, Taiwan, the Philippines, and other Far Eastern countries.[73] Figures vary and are growing, but pirated and smuggled videocassettes probably hold about $2 billion worth, or one-eighth of the $16 billion international faked goods business.[74]*

Lest it seem that all videocassettes are pirated, or all uses illegal, it should be stressed that there is, of course, a giant and rapidly growing legitimate videocassette market.[75] But, while publicity usually focuses on economic factors, the main political point is that this software is frequently not susceptible even to the brakes applied by the usual market forces. Whatever type of video programming is wanted by individuals, wherever in the world it is wanted, it is either readily available or usually fairly easily obtainable — regardless of a government's wishes — under the present distribution system.

---

* Pirated videocassettes are not "faked" goods, in the sense that they are copies of "real" films, etc. But their distributors are not legitimate.

NOTES

[1]Multiple references concerning many countries attest to the described development.

[2]Eric Gelman et al., "The Video Revolution," *Newsweek,* August 6, 1984, p. 52, and others.

[3]Robert Trumbull, "Videotapes of Slaying Smuggled Into Manila," *The New York Times,* September 13, 1983, p. A-9.

"U.S. Filipinos Sending Home Published Attacks on Marcos," *The New York Times,* February 7, 1984, p. A-10.

[4]"Customs Cannot Stem Imports of Video Porn, Bussieres Admits," *Montreal Gazette,* February 15, 1983, p. B-1.

[5]Javed Jabbar, "Pakistan. A Cautious Welcome," *InterMedia,* July/September 1983, pp. 65-66.

For an impassioned plea by a citizen for government control of Indian films in Pakistan, see: "Press Plea to Stop Illegal Flood of Indian Films," *Pakistan Series, Public Opinion Trends, Analyses and News Service* (POT), Volume XIII, No. 175, September 19, 1985, pp. 3348-3349.

[6]Emel Anil, "Bootleg Movies Are Big Business in Turkey," *The Associated Press,* February 28, 1984 (NEXIS).

[7]*Ibid.*

[8]*Ibid.*

[9]Anna Christensen, "The Black Sea: Prostitution and Punks," *United Press International,* August 19, 1984 (NEXIS).

[10]Donald R. Shanor, *Behind the Lines. The Private War Against Soviet Censorship.* St. Martin's Press, New York, 1985, p. 154.

[11]*Ibid.,* p. 154.

[12]Philip Taubman, "Oh Comrade, Can I Borrow Your Rambo Cassette?" *The New York Times,* December 9, 1985, p. A-2.

[13]*Ibid.*

[14]"Rushin' to Their VCRs," *TV Guide,* Volume 33, Number 17, April 27/May 3, 1985, p. A-2.

[15]Ben Wattenberg, "VCR, The Ultimate Weapon," *The Washington Times,* November 21, 1985, p. D-1.

Edmund Stevens, "Video Vice That Spelt Ruin for Piano Professor," *Sunday Times* of London, October 13, 1985, p. 10.

Philip Taubman, "Soviet Pans 'Rocky' and 'Rambo' Films," *The New York Times,* January 4, 1986, p. A-3.

[16]Philip Taubman, "Oh Comrade, Can I Borrow Your Rambo Cassette?" *The New York Times,* December 9, 1985, p. A-2.

[17]Douglas Stanglin. Personal communications.

[18]*Ibid.*

[19]*Ibid.*

[20]*Ibid.*

[21]Czechoslovakia. Personal communications.

[22]"Prague Steps Up Output of Video Recorders," *Soviet East European Report,* Radio Free Europe/Radio Liberty, Volume II, No. 25, June 10, 1985, p. 2.

V. S., "On the Verge of the Video Revolution," Situation Report, Czechoslovakia/9, *Radio Free Europe Research,* Radio Free Europe-Radio Liberty, June 3, 1985, pp. 31-33.

[23]George Jahn, "Video Cassette Black Market Flourishes in Hungary, *The Associated Press,* April 26, 1985 (NEXIS).

[24]Steven Koppany, "Unprepared Regime Scrambles to Meet Challenges of the Video Era," Situation Report, Hungary/10, *Radio Free Europe Research,* Radio Free Europe-Radio Liberty, September 4, 1985, p. 19.

The Radio Free Europe-Radio Liberty reports on Bulgaria, Hungary, Czechoslovakia, and Poland cited in this and/or other chapters of this paper should be read in their entirety for a good overview of the Eastern European VCR/cassette situation.

[25]*Ibid.*, p. 20.

[26]Michael Cieply, "Film-Studio 'Cop' Acts to Foil Latin Pirates of U.S. Hit Movies," *The Wall Street Journal*, April 19, 1985, p. 1.

[27]"Central America in Brief," *Variety*, March 20, 1985, p. 46.

[28]"South Africa Blocks Olympics TV Viewing," *Variety*, August 15, 1984, p. 2.

"Index Index. South Africa." *Index on Censorship*, Volume 13, Number 6, December 1984, p. 48.

"Politics in the Press Box," *Manchester Guardian Weekly*, July 29, 1984, p. 1.

[29]"Central America in Brief," *Variety*, March 20, 1985, p. 46.

[30]Michael Cieply, "Film Studio 'Cop' Acts to Fail Latin Pirates of U.S. Hit Movies," *The Wall Street Journal*, April 19, 1985, p. 16.

[31]Paul Lenti, "Importation Ban on Homevideo Has Led to a Plague in Mexico of Widespread Piracy, Smuggling," *Variety*, March 27, 1985, p. 34.

[32]Peter Besas, " 'Legal' Homevid in Latino Orbit. Huge Potential from a New Territory," *Variety*, March 20, 1985, p. 61.

[33]"Pirate Vid Haul in West Africa Includes U.S. Tapes," *Variety*, October 3, 1984, p. 2.

[34]*Ibid.*

[35]Peter Hulm, "Dateline: Geneva," *Reuters*, March 25, 1981 (NEXIS).

[36]"Pirate Vid Haul in West Africa Includes U.S. Tapes," *Variety*, October 3, 1984, p. 2.

[37]Michael Duggan, "Dateline: London," *Reuters*, December 17, 1982, (NEXIS).

[38]"Effective Gains Made by FACT vs. U.K. Pirates," *Variety*, January 23, 1985, p. 41.

[39]Ed Blanche, "Movie Men Go Gunning for Video Pirates," December 22, 1982, *The Associated Press* (NEXIS).

[40]"Pirates of Singapore Elbow Legit Ops Aside," *Variety*, October 10, 1984, p. 82.

[41]David Fouquet, "Pirated Movies From Out-of-the-way Places," *The Christian Science Monitor*, March 4, 1983, p. 5.

[42]"Pirates Go Undercover," *Variety*, October 17, 1984, p. 41.

See also:

"Pirates on Wheels," *Variety*, June 19, 1985, p. 42, which mentions British pirates who tour the country, operating from trucks and converted ambulances.

[43]David Kline, "Asia's 'Golden Crescent' Heroin Floods the West," *The Christian Science Monitor*, November 9, 1982, p. 1 (NEXIS).

David W. Willis, "Paradoxical Pakistan; Camels and Color TV, Nuclear Power and 'Nationalized Corruption'," *The Christian Science Monitor*, November 25, 1981, p. B-12.

"Dateline: Islamabad, Pakistan," *The Associated Press*, January 6, 1981.

[44]Peter Hulm, "Dateline: Geneva," *Reuters*, March 25, 1981 (NEXIS).

[45]*Ibid.*

[46]*Ibid.*

[47]Richard Klein, "Pic Assn.'s Nix Gives Antipiracy Advice to Members of AFMA," *Variety*, December 12, 1984, p. 6.

[48]Ed Blanche, "Movie Men Go Gunning for Video Pirates," *The Associated Press*, December 22, 1982 (NEXIS).

[49]*Organized Crime. Report of the Task Force on Organized Crime*. National Advisory Committee on Criminal Justice Standards and Goals: 1976. Department of Justice, Washington, DC, 1976, pp. 226–227.

[50]*Ibid.*

[51]*Ibid.*

[52]"Chicago Boothmen's Local Has History of Mob Connections," *Variety,* April 17, 1985, pp. 6, 20.

[53]*Ibid.,* p. 20.

[54]*Ibid.*

[55]*Ibid.*

[56]Robert D. McFadden, "New York Pornography Suspect Dies as Agents Seek Him," *The New York Times,* February 15, 1980, p. B-4.

[57]*Ibid.*

[58]*Ibid.*

[59]Bob Jamison, *NBC Nightly News,* February 28, 1984 (and newspaper articles).

[60]"Sketches of 9 Arrested," *The Boston Globe,* February 27, 1985, p. 2. And many others.

[61]"Sketches of 9 Arrested," *The Boston Globe,* February 27, 1985, p. 2.

[62]Stanley Penn, "Alleged Heads of Mafia Groups Charged by U.S.", *The Wall Street Journal,* February 27, 1985, p. 7.

[63]Robert Lindsey, "Officials Challenge Outlets That Offer Explicit Videotapes," *The New York Times,* June 3, 1985, p. B-14.

[64]*Ibid.*

[65]*Ibid.*

[66]Christopher McCooey, "The Yakuza's Lucrative Traffic in Guns, Drugs and Girls," *Far Eastern Economic Review,* September 27, 1984, pp. 61–62.

Melinda Beck, Martin Kasindorf, Kim Willenson, and Mary Lord, "The Yakuza Connection," *Newsweek,* January 11, 1982, p. 25.

See also for growing concerns regarding crime groups:

Sam Roberts, "A Profile of the American Mafia: Old Bosses and New Competitors. A Dying Breed of Leaders," *The New York Times,* October 4, 1984, pp. 1, B-12.

"Int'l Anti-Piracy Gets Review," *Variety,* October 10, 1984, p. 1.

[67]Hazel Guild, "German Authorities Keep Pressure on Vid Pirates As Stakes Grow Higher," *Variety,* January 23, 1985, p. 43.

[68]*Ibid.*

[69]"Int'l. Anti-Piracy Gets Review," *Variety,* October 10, 1984, p. 1.

[70]"Most Obscenity Seized at Border Features Youth," *The New York Times,* July 28, 1982, p. B-22.

[71]Yehai Aboubakr, "Egypt. Late Arrivals," *InterMedia,* July/September, 1983, p. 48.

[72]Ronald Taylor, "Business Goes After Fake Goods for Real," *U.S. News & World Report,* June 13, 1983, p. 76.

[73]*Ibid.*

[74]*Ibid.,* and also:

Robert Arnold Russel, "In Defense of Piracy," *Executive,* September 1983, pp. 47–48.

James Fleming, "The Menace of Bogus Brands," *Maclean's,* February 18, 1985, pp. 34–35.

Tyler Marshall, "A Deluge of Phony Books. Worldwide Piracy Costs Legitimate Companies Billions," *The Boston Globe,* October 28, 1984, pp. 61, 63.

[75]"Kaupe: U.S. Mart Dominates the World," *Variety,* November 28, 1984, p. 82.

CHAPTER SEVEN

What People Are Watching and Where They Are Watching It

People the world over have welcomed VCRs and cassettes in every country we have considered. Little or no thought about whether they are legal appears to have been given, except for devising ways to get around governmental restrictions. What people are watching, in general, is whatever amuses or informs them. This includes comedies, adventure, action films, documentaries, all sorts of feature films and television programs, and kiddie fare, as well as "video nasties" and pornography. It also includes material that is subtly or not so subtly political.[1]

First-run American films and television programming are among the "best sellers." All Western films and programming, of whatever vintage, are popular. Ex-British colonials often prefer British films and programming. English-language films in general are highly sought after, since this is the language most widely comprehended. French films and programming are favored in all the French-speaking countries. The U.S. is gaining access to quite a lot of foreign films via videocassette. In mid-1984, for example, *Video Movies* magazine listed 69 French language films available in the U.S. on video,[2] and, in early 1986, in Harvard Square, Cambridge, for instance, Video Biz was offering about 80 foreign films in its catalog of just under 1000 selections.[3] Italian and German and other European films are watched widely. Hong Kong films have a big audience beyond Chinese-speaking populations. Videocassettes have increased the access to what people prefer to watch anyway, and in most cases have greatly increased the variety.

Egypt, as the "cultural capital" of the Arab world, is the source of many films and dramas which circulate in the Middle East. Egypt makes as much on videocassette rights as it does on movies. Indeed, because "in the Arab gulf and Saudi Arabia, there are no public theaters . . . videocassettes are the main method of distribution."[4] Egyptian and other Middle Eastern plays are often very political, using satirical comedy to criticize the government and society. The *Index on Censorship* reports:

> Every popular play is . . . recorded on video tapes, and many on [audio] cassettes. Villagers in Upper Egypt, Bedouins in Saudi Arabia or Dubai, fishermen in Iraq, all see Egyptian, Syrian, and Kuwaiti popular plays without having to know what a theatre looks like. . . .[5]

An extremely famous Egyptian play is cited as typical of the political orientation. *The Witness Who Witnessed Nothing* was banned by Sadat and is still kept off Egyptian TV. The play was, however, broadcast by the other Arab nations repeatedly following the falling-out with Egypt over the Camp David agreement with Israel. Says the *Index on Censorship:*

> nowadays, no Arab video library is complete without it. Children know the lines by heart. The plot concerns an average citizen who is called to testify about the murder of his neighbour. In court, the relationship between citizen and state is revealed: the witness shows total ignorance of everything except the overpowering presence of the state in every aspect of life. Giving evidence in the murder trial he declares that "there is no housing shortage, no public transportation problems, and . . . long live the government. . . ."[6]

A similarly political Lebanese musical called *The Keeper of the Keys* circulates on audiocassette.[7]

In 1984, Egypt took offense at the "Sadat" miniseries and banned it and any other films produced or distributed by Columbia Pictures. *The New York Times* said

> objections to the film, starring . . . [Louis Gossett, Jr.] who won an Oscar for his performance in "An Officer and a Gentleman," are complex. They range from resentment in some circles over the selection of a black to play Mr. Sadat, to often cited objections concerning "distortions" of Egyptian leaders and life, to historical inaccuracies.[8]

The *Times* also reported that,

> before 1979, when Egypt signed a peace treaty with Israel, foreign actors, actresses and film companies that were prominent in their support of Israel were frequently banned in Egypt . . . [9]

Since the treaty, this response has eased, but the "Sadat" banning upset the Israelis, already worried about their strained Egyptian relations. The editor-in-chief of *Al Akhbar,* a major Cairo newspaper, did not allay these worries when he editorialized that "the film 'Sadat' . . . was a plot by 'evil Zionist powers.' "[10] "Sadat" circulates freely on pirated videocassettes in Egypt, but those who view it are said not to like it.[11]* Egyptians are said mainly to prefer uncensored versions of their own Egyptian movies and plays, obtained by smuggling the master out of the country and then re-smuggling the uncensored copies back in.[13]

---

* Boyd and Straubhaar say that the available Sadat video is "the result of dubbed copies of a single cassette recorded directly from U.S. television."[12]

Hindi and other Indian films are tremendously popular, not only in India but also in the Middle East — even though most people don't understand the language.[14] Hindi films are also widely watched where they are banned — in Pakistan and Bangladesh. *InterMedia* describes the weekly police raids in Karachi, Pakistan, of commercial showings of Indian films, saying

> sometimes, the evening papers publish pictures of the organizers being arrested, doing their best to look ashamed, and failing in the attempt. For it is public knowledge that virtually every house which has a VCR machine (and in the major cities and towns every second home in every high income and every upper middle class neighbourhood/area probably has a VCR set) is bound to be screening an Indian movie at one time or another without suffering any police raid.[15]

The police are said to intervene only when the offense becomes too blatant. In Bangladesh:

> illegal VTRs of Indian movies, which are not allowed . . . and uncensored Western films some of which may be pornographic by even Western standards, are freely available. . . .[16]

The movie "Gandhi" "has not been permitted in Pakistan movie houses,"[17] because it is felt that the role of Mohammed Ali Jinnah, Pakistan's founder, was badly slighted in favor of Gandhi. The film is, however, illegally "available on videocassette, and private showings have become a common form of at-home entertainment."[18] Turkey has also banned "Gandhi," "under pressure from Pakistan, a good friend. . . ."[19] But in early 1984, "Gandhi" was circulating in Turkey on videocassette, along with "Return of the Jedi," "E.T.," "Sophie's Choice," and "The Day After."* Most of the VCRs (said to number about a million) and the tapes have come into Turkey illegally. The few films on Turkish TV are mainly old black and whites. Movies are censored, and arrive in Turkey only two to four years after release in the U.S. and Europe.

The ineffectiveness of Ayatollah Khomeini's ban on VCRs and cassettes can be seen in the following quotations:

> VCRs and cassettes are banned in Iran, but thousands have been smuggled in by wealthy Iranians. . . .[21]

---

* It is said that these videos and much off-the-air European television programming are obtained from London, Paris, and Brussels-based pirates, and then "Turks living or traveling abroad carry them to their homeland."[20] When the United States Information Agency (USIA) offered a private screening of "The Day After" as a special treat for a selected group in Turkey, most of the guests had already seen it.

In . . . Iran, not even the hate-America policy of current political leaders has dampened the demand for Hollywood products . . . although U.S. movies have virtually disappeared from Iran's movie houses, American films such as "E.T." are widely available for home viewing in videocassettes.[22]

. . . unofficial "video shops," selling cassettes of Western films, are one of the few booming businesses in Tehran. In a north Tehran apartment one night, a reporter found two teen-age boys and two girls huddled around a videocassette recorder watching "One Flew Over the Cuckoo's Nest."

Not only would the mullahs have frowned on the film, but the gathering itself was illicit — putting boys and veil-less girls together is an offense punishable by a dozen or more lashes. . . .[23]

. . . Everybody seems to have a video-recorder, and copies of American videocassettes are easily available. This correspondent was the only guest at a party not to have seen Michael Jackson's *Thriller* video.[24]

In September 1985, an unclassified United States Information Agency (USIA) cable reported, regarding Iran.:

As a result of strict control over films shown in public theaters, an enormous black market in video cassettes has come into existence to provide western films for a high price to the middle and upper classes. Here one can rent or buy most of the films that are currently available in the west . . . According to a participant in the black market, the most popular films in Iran today are "Footloose" (which deals in part with rebellion against fundamental religious principles) and "The Return of the Jedi" (which is politically controversial as many Iranians have compared Khomeini to the evil and aging emperor of dark forces portrayed in the film). . . .[25]

Rock video and porno are also said to be popular in Iran.

Penalties for unauthorized use of videocassettes are more severe in Iran than in any other country seen in this study. The same cable reported that

importation or possession of all videocassettes not approved by the government (i.e. films not currently being offered to Iranian theaters) is illegal and we have been told that arrests for this activity are numerous. Penalties vary considerably ranging from two to twelve months incarceration to death . . . [26]

One black marketeer, says the cable, was beheaded in 1984 for selling copies of a hard-core pornographic film.

Reports on what is being watched in the USSR have surfaced in many sources. As has been discussed, much entertainment and news is taped in Estonia from Finnish television,[27] but pornography and many Western films are also being smuggled into Russia. Tapes are regularly borrowed by Rus-

sians from the tape libraries of resident foreigners — diplomats, correspond-
ents, and businessmen.[28] Some tapes are being shown by VCR-owning Soviet "entrepreneurs" for big money. *Reuters* says

> when the midnight video show began at a sleazy bar on the Soviet Union's
> Black Sea coast, the customers knew what to expect — "sex, supermen and
> sadism."

> At $70 a head, the audience was guaranteed the latest in Western pornogra-
> phy, supplied by an underground syndicate based in Moscow.[29]

V. Sevryugov, the boss of this syndicate, is said to have been arrested and
sentenced to eight years in prison. According to *Reuters:*

> Sovietskaya Rossiya [which announced the arrest] said the West was trying to
> encourage circulation of uncensored films among impressionable Soviet audi-
> ences in order to undermine Communist morality.[30]

That Russian newspaper also was reported as saying "the films shown sometimes included 'open slander on our history and our current policies' . . . "[31]
Despite the arrest of this syndicate boss, Russians say that "western videotapes are still in wide circulation in Moscow and there are underground
libraries which hire out uncensored films."[32] These tapes are often shown in
private apartments, by invitation, to people who pay 5 or more rubles each
for the privilege of seeing them. *U.S. News and World Report* says:

> on the Moscow black market, a Jane Fonda workout tape sells for $372, and an
> original tape of an American Western movie is priced at $250 to $300. Asian
> entrepreneurs, especially Hong Kong, are dubbing into Russian such tapes as
> those of Bruce Lee karate films for the incipient Soviet market.[33]

The New York Times reported in 1983 that

> among Moscow's cognoscenti, a sort of hit parade of most-desired movies has
> developed. The favorites include "One Flew Over the Cuckoo's Nest" . . .
> "The Deer Hunter," "Apocalypse Now," "Last Tango in Paris," "A Clockwork
> Orange," "Straw Dogs," and "The Godfather."[34]

By 1985, the Soviet black market "best sellers" included "Rambo," "Ama-
deus," and Poland's "Man of Iron," the latter a film "that sympathetically
chronicles labor unrest in Gdansk, the birthplace of the Solidarity labor union movement."[35] The Soviets are also said to enjoy movies like "April in
Paris" or "Christmas in Bavaria" and James Bond films, or whatever gives
them

relief from the tiresome diet of uplifting discussions, war movies . . . the strug-
gles to get the dam built, the land plowed, and the production quota met . . . [36]

In short, they like the possibility of watching "for half an hour or an entire
evening without feeling preached to. . . ."[37] The Soviet authorities object to
even such seemingly innocuous entertainment, for

> there is no such thing as a neutral story, Soviet ideologists contend. Western
> filmmakers may pretend or even believe that they have no political message,
> but they are wrong, according to the Soviet critic Grigory Oganov: "When a
> nice-looking modern Cinderella with whom millions of young girls can easily
> identify themselves finds her capitalist wonderland prince; or when the cruel
> policeman of a TV serial is made into a public hero, when a wicked spy and
> killer is glorified as a rescuer of civilization, there is yet another juggling trick,
> where notions are manipulated like cards. That is how anti-Sovietism is being
> whipped up."[38]*

Less innocently, Soviets are also interested in "anti-Soviet" films like " 'Dr.
Zhivago,' or film versions of works by Alexander Solzhenitsyn."[41] A 1982 article reported:

> it is thought that the main danger posed by video is in the showing of the sort of
> television documentaries and discussion programs about foreign affairs and
> Soviet internal policies that are not shown on Soviet television. [42]

While originally confined to a small group of elites — privileged officials,
artists, etc. — videocassettes are now said to be "filtering in via the black market, enabling others [than high officials, etc.] to screen private showings of
banned films across the country."[43] The children of the privileged elites, "the
Zolotaya Molodyozh, or Golden Youth,"[44] are also active in watching (and
probably sharing) video. *The Christian Science Monitor* reported in May 1983
that *Sovietskaya Rossiya*

> recently suggested the video circle has widened . . . [and] spoke of illegal cas-
> sette sales from Odessa to Leningrad, and of private showings "in apartments
> or closed cafes after work hours."[45]

---

* Indonesia's former leader, Achmed Sukarno, is credited with remarking that: "U.S. film
producers were revolutionaries because they featured refrigerators in films shown in his country, and these appliances were very attractive to those living in a hot climate."[39] The late India
Prime Minister Indira Ghandi made a similar comment: " 'A refrigerator seen on a comedy television show can become a revolutionary symbol to the deprived villager' . . . "[40] The sight of su-
permarkets piled high with food and new cars carelessly being demolished are often mentioned
as main attractions in American movies.

Massachusetts Institute of Technology Professor Loren Graham plays down the political importance of either audio or videocassettes in the USSR, saying that the printing press remains the principal Soviet political medium. Audiocassettes, he says, are used primarily for music, which may be "mildly subversive." Videocassettes, he says, are mainly devoted to pornography.[46] Professor Graham also says that the Soviets have videocassettes well under control. But Donald Shanor points to an overall lack of control by authorities, as well a some uses of videocassettes for magnitizdat.[47]

The Soviets have been trying to scare people away from watching videocassettes — in one instance by citing "a woman who ended up in a mental hospital after viewing horror movies. . . ."[48] Some version of this crackup-after-viewing-an-"undesirable"-tape story is making the rounds in several countries. In Jordan, for instance:

> According to [a] psychiatrist . . . this sudden exposure to such films in a conservative society could definitely create psychiatric problems, especially among teenage Jordanians. An incident has already occurred to a 16-year-old girl who innocently invited her friends to watch a nice video movie, which turned out to be a porno one. Apparently her brother had not bothered to hide it in a safe place and she saw it by mistake which caused her a nervous breakdown and hospitalization.[49]

This is apparently the video culture's version of the old-fashioned masturbation-will-make-you-crazy morality story.

The Polish government claims to have a monopoly on videocassettes under a "1958 Act . . . establishing a state monopoly for the public distribution of all visual recordings. . . ."[50] It appears to rationalize permitting some VCRs, since there is this supposed "safety net" on programming. In January 1981, a Polish film, "Workers '80," "a documentary account of the [1980] 16 day strike in the Gdansk shipyards" was the hottest film in Warsaw. It was not banned, but neither was it formally approved for showing. *The New York Times* said it had been quietly shown in a few Warsaw theaters, and that "videotape versions are circulating among select audiences."[51] Solidarity was then in full swing, but the *Times* reported that the film was severely criticized by the *Trybuna Ludu,* the Communist Party newspaper.[52]

Prior to the imposition of martial law, there were student video clubs in the larger Polish cities showing "Polish language versions of Western films that lacked a license for official circulation."[53] These videocassettes were said to have come from the private collection of Maciej Szczepanski, the former boss of the Radio and Television Committee.[54] In January 1984, after a two-year trial for "irregularities in managing the state's financial resources," Szczepanski was sentenced to eight years in prison "for enriching himself at the state's expense while . . . in charge of Poland's official radio and television."[55] Szczepanski was linked politically to Edward Gierek, who is said to have led Poland to economic disaster. Szczepanski

> admitted cutting corners and ignoring bureaucratic regulations, but said he was innocent of the main charges . . . [and was being] made a political scapegoat. . . .[56]

Although they were not mentioned during the trial,

> a series of lurid exposes about the excesses of Szczepanski and his associates told of a network of private resorts around the country and abroad, a yacht so lavish that it was equipped with stables, a secret videotape library of x-rated films and a brothel reserved for TV executives.[57]

UPI says the Poles remember Szczepanski best "for his television programming, which included scores of Western films, musicals, cabarets and variety shows."[58]

Although audiocassettes were much more prevalent, videocassettes were also used to a certain extent by Solidarity in both its heyday and it post-crackdown activities. In 1983, *The Washington Post* reported that Solidarity activists,

> taunting the authorities by their ability to operate under the nose of the police . . . managed this month to videotape, then smuggled to the West, an interview with Poland's most wanted leader in hiding, Zbigniew Bujak, former head of Solidarity's Warsaw Branch.[59]

Radio Free Europe said, in May 1985, "the Polish underground has recently added video recording to its many means of fighting censorship."[60] Poland's oldest underground publishing house, NOWa, established in 1977, which has already published "about 200 books" and "more than 17 sound cassettes," has begun a new activity: "A special unit has been set up specializing in the mass production of video cassettes for independent circulation."[61] In addition, *Radio Free Europe* quoted Tygodnik Mazowsze, an underground weekly in and around Warsaw, as saying:

> "amateur, independent movie-making is emerging — after all, anyone can make a video film, no special studios and laboratories are needed. Churches show video films of the funerals of Father Popieluszko and Grzegorz Przemyk, and at private showings one can see Danuta Walesa accepting the Nobel Peace Prize '(on behalf of her husband),' or the British television film on Solidarity called *Squaring the Circle,* or Bugajski's *The Interrogation.* Recently, a documentary was made of an exhibition shown in the Holy Cross Church in Warsaw and called 'The Apocalypse — A Light in Darkness.' The exhibition was visited

by Bishop Miziolek and the camera accompanied him, filming the whole exhibition. There is no doubt that a quantum leap can be expected in this area; at present video films are still an exclusive facility in Poland."[62]

NOWa talks of possibly extending its videotaping facilities to independent movie makers.

Group showings of videos in homes are commonplace in many countries, including the U.S. In Israel, group viewing is said to be "reminiscent of the early days of television."[63] In Egypt, groups often meet in homes, sharing expenses for food and video rental. This also happens regularly in India. In Sri Lanka, videos are usually watched by families as a whole, or with friends and neighbors, but

> in some households it is not unusual to find a fee being charged; for some, screening videos for a fee has become good business, although it is contrary to the Entertainment Tax regulations.[64]

In India, videos are not only popular at parties, but at least 50,000 illegal video "parlors" in private homes are said to have sprung up. Here, three or four shows daily are presented to groups of 25 or 30 for an admission of pennies. This is taking place all over India, from the large city slums to the small towns and even villages. A minimum of 400 towns and villages are said to have already been "invaded" by these parlors. Bombay's worst slum is said to have at least 30.[65] In Bangladesh, "many of the exclusive clubs [around Dacca] have regular 'movie nights' when . . . smuggled [Hindi and Pakistani] films are shown to members."[66] In Burma, the media is "ruthlessly controlled,"[67] and "no foreign books have been legally imported . . . [for] two decades. . . ." There are, in addition, "no nightclubs, a bottle of Mandalay beer costs too much for most Burmese, and restaurants close around 9 p.m."[68]

There are, however, "special television houses" where videocassettes can be seen for about a dollar.[69] In the Guangdong Province of China, peasants have set up "makeshift theaters . . . to show raunchy videotapes smuggled in from Hong Kong. . . ."[70] In the same province, many peasants have also "put up UHF 'fishbone' antennas to bring in sassy television shows from Hong Kong, despite periodic campaigns by the authorities to pull them down. . . ."[71] *Time* says,

> in some video parlors, where impromptu movie screenings are shown with a video recorder, customers pay 30 times as much to see an imported pornographic movie as a Chinese film. . . .[72]

Under pressure by IFPI, the Chinese authorities have been attempting to "curb unauthorized video use."[73] *Variety*, in fall 1985, reported that "20,000 semi-public halls that charged entrance fees to video viewers have been closed down by CITV [China International Television Corporation]."[74] The article said,

> communal video viewing . . . will be allowed, but notices will be placed at the beginning of all imported tapes calling on audiences to report any entrance charges to the authorities.[75]

Faced with a need to keep the increasingly "rich" peasants amused, and especially to keep them from going to the cities, the Chinese government is encouraging peasants themselves to develop "cultural households."[76] In the provinces of Liaoning, Hebei, Hubei, Anbui, and Shandong, "incomplete statistics" show 130,000 peasants engaging in "cultural business instead of farming."[77] In addition to showing videotapes, these activities promoted by the Ministry of Culture include cinemas, theaters, drama troupes, libraries, photo studios, and fine arts services. Many have become multi-functional. For instance,

> Shuai Chengguang, a peasant in Hanshou County, Hunan Province, runs a culture center in his village. He erected a two-story building which has a library with a collection of more than 2,000 books, a television room with 1000 seats, a musical tea-house with 64 seats and a recreation room equipped with billiards, chess, cards and so on. His customers can spend an entertaining day at the center by paying only a few cents.[78]

In Israel, 50% of the kibbutzim are said to be either wired for cable "or to have strategically placed VCR sets offering an alternative to Israeli broadcasts. . . ."[79] In Great Britain, many pubs and clubs have legal video,[80] but, in South Korea and in Iran, videos are often illegally shown in coffee houses.[81]

Underground video parlors are making great inroads in Eastern Europe. In Hungary, where black marketeers will make prints of videocassettes for customers for $6 or $7, using the customer's blank tape, "road shows" are popular. The customers take their VCRs " 'to some state-run factory club or one run by the Organization of Young Communists and play what they just got recorded'. . . ."[82] Some previously approved and advertised film is displaced to accommodate the videocassette. *The Associated Press* was told that " 'It's possible to earn more than 30,000 forints ($600) a month this way.' "[83] In Bulgaria, where tapes " ' . . . shot . . . in basements and bordellos between Istanbul and Calcutta' "[84] can be obtained from foreign truck drivers passing through, arrests for "possessing 'unearned income' or engaging in unauthorized private enterprise" involving showing videocassettes are prevalent.[85] One family "had torn down the walls of their apartment" to accommodate up to 50 people a showing.[86] Also, in Bulgaria:

> apart from purely private video clubs, there are semiofficial video cinemas. A person or a group owning a video set and tapes leases them to a coffee shop, bar, or restaurant and gets, as a rule, tax-free remuneration.[87]

Videocassettes have become very mobile. Most international airlines are switching from movies to video. France has put video on one coach of the main East/West Paris subway line.[88] The London to Glasgow Express train got a video viewing coach in November 1984, with "Tootsie" and "Police Academy" as the first showings.[89] Indians choose buses depending on what videocassette is being shown.[90] In Scotland, bus companies rented by football supporters' clubs and other groups for awhile showed videocassettes in transit. Because they hired cassettes for $4 a day "rather than concluding more expensive licensing,"[91] they became the target of the FACT copyright policing operatives. And in Turkey, during a price war between transit lines, interacity buses "boosted ridership by showing videocassette films. . . ."[92] These were discontinued because there were protests from the film industry, and also because "passengers complained about bus drivers watching the films."[93]

An interesting mobile use of videos was reported by *BBC Summary of World Broadcasts* for Poland:

> More than half of the vessels used by the Polish Shipping Company (PZM) possess video recorders and special TV sets which make it possible to receive programmes from all the systems in use throughout the world. Pre-recorded cassettes can be exchanged when the ships return to Poland. Other ship owners are keen to follow PZM's example; Polish Ocean Lines (PLO) have purchased 35 units at a cost of about 4,000 dollars each, which will be used shortly to relay specialized educational and shipping programmes.[94]

VCRs are used the world over for time shifting and for taping off-the-air programming. Video cameras are widely employed to record family events like weddings. However, it is said for Jamaica that

> an increasing number of residents and organisations are now acquiring ½-inch cameras for use with the VHS recorders, and are making their own programmes for training, entertainment, guidance, and counselling. This opens new avenues for professional film-makers and suggests that at last the expensive communications systems of the elite are beginning to reach the masses who most need education, information and a pride in their own heritage.[95]

This would seem to go well beyond the institutional and educational uses that are, of course, being made of VCRs and cassettes in many countries, to a variety of uses by individuals.

Teenagers in London have taken a very creative approach to video production through a technique called "scratching." The *Observer* reported in spring 1984 that

> fast, rough and exciting, video scratching is the latest thing in street sound and vision. In the clubs, scratch DJs mix together their own music from other people's records. Now, young video scratchers are mixing together pictures on their ordinary home televisions and video recorders to make scratch video tapes. By plugging a musicassette player into the "audio dub" socket of a VCR, they tape their own taped music on to a video tape. At the same time, they pick their own pictures to match the music.[96]

Various techniques can be used for "scratching":

> The simplest scratch technique is to switch between channels in time with the music. This produces a set of jumping, jolting, random pictures, changing with the beat. It's up to the scratcher to pick the most interesting programmes, and to change channels at just the right time.[97]

A more advanced technique, using one VCR, is to tape a continuous piece of some program, pick out a point in this to drop in something else, and, by holding the recorder on "pause," find another interesting piece on TV for recording. When all the visuals have been completed, suitable music can be added.

There is an even more sophisticated method:

> By using a second VCR, serious scratchers can keep a store of pictures, instead of waiting for the right thing to appear on TV. "Then you can pre-plan your tapes," says Charlie Whittock, who has mixed nuclear test footage in with the old film, "The Day The Earth Stood Still," over George Clinton's single "Atomic Dog." "You can use images that really mean something to you."[98]

In short, these teenagers are the VCR equivalents of today's army of computer hackers.

NOTES

[1]Many sources, including most of the references in this chapter.

[2]Matthew White and Darrell Moore, "Bastille Day Marathon. 24 Hours of French Movies," *Video Movies,* July 1984, pp. 35–38.

[3]Personal observation. The authors.

[4]Mounir B. Abboud, "Egyptian Pictures Still Pack in Arabs in Spite of Politics," *Variety,* October 31, 1984, p. 6.

[5]"Middle Eastern Story-tellers Give Way to Videos," *Index on Censorship,* Volume 14, Number 1, February 1985, p. 53.

[6]*Ibid.*

[7]*Ibid.*

[8]Judith Miller, "Upset by 'Sadat', Egypt Bars Columbia Films," *The New York Times,* February 2, 1984, p. A-1.

[9]*Ibid.*

[10]*Ibid.*

[11]*Ibid.*

[12]Douglas A. Boyd and Joseph D. Straubhaar, "Developmental Impact of the Home Video Cassette Recorder on Third World Countries," *Journal of Broadcasting & Electronic Media,* Volume 29, Number 1, Winter 1985, p. 12.

[13]Yehia Aboubakr, "Egypt. Late Arrivals," *InterMedia,* July/September, 1983, p. 48.

[14]T. N. Ninan and Chander Uday Singh, "India's Entertainment Revolution," *World Press Review,* September 1983, p. 58.

[15]Javed Jabbar, "Pakistan. A Cautious Welcome," *InterMedia,* July/September, 1983, pp. 65–66.

[16]Bangladesh. Personal communications.

[17]Sidharth Bhatia, "Dateline: Bombay," *The Associated Press,* July 12, 1983 (NEXIS).

[18]Richard Bill, "Dateline: Islamabad," *The Associated Press,* April 25, 1983 (NEXIS).

[19]Emel Anil, "Bootleg Movies Are Big Business in Turkey," *The Associated Press,* February 28, 1984 (NEXIS).

[20]*Ibid.*

[21]"VCRs Go on Fast Forward. Proliferating Players and Tapes Spread Western Fare Worldwide," *Time,* December 13, 1982, p. 78.

[22]"Out of Reach of the Curious Censors," *U.S. News & World Report,* July 23, 1984, p. 46.

[23]Charles J. Hanley, "In the Age of Khomeini, Tehran Moves at Half-Step," *The Associated Press,* November 23, 1982 (NEXIS).

[24]"Iran. Tehran Accomodates," *World Press Review,* November 1984, p. 55. Reprinted from *The Economist.*

[25]"Censorship and Entertainment in Iran," United States Information Agency (USIA) unclassified cable, U.S. Department of State from the U.S. Mission, Berlin, September 1985.

[26]*Ibid.,* and also:

"Iran Cracks Down," *Variety,* February 19, 1986, p. 4.

[27]Donald R. Shanor, *Behind the Lines. The Private War Against Soviet Censorship.* St. Martin's Press, New York, 1985, p. 154.

[28]*Ibid.,* p. 157.

[29]John Morrison, "Soviet-Pornography. Dateline: Moscow," *Reuters,* August 24, 1983 (NEXIS).

[30]*Ibid.*

[31]*Ibid.,* and also:

Serge Schmemann, "Video's Forbidden Offerings Alarm Moscow," *The New York Times,* October 22, 1983, p. A-1.

[32]John Morrison, "Soviet-Pornography, "Dateline: Moscow," *Reuters,* August 24, 1983, (NEXIS).

[33]"Out of Reach of the Curious Censors," *U.S. News & World Report,* July 23, 1984, p. 46.

[34]Serge Schmemann, "Video's Forbidden Offerings Alarm Moscow," *The New York Times,* October 22, 1983, p. A-1.

[35]Philip Taubman, "Oh Comrade, Can I Borrow Your Rambo Cassette?" *The New York Times,* December 9, 1985, p. A-2.

See also:

Philip Taubman, "Soviet Pans 'Rocky' and 'Rambo' Films," *The New York Times,* January 4, 1986, p. A-3.

[36]Donald R. Shanor, *Behind the Lines. The Private War Against Soviet Censorship.*, St. Martin's Press, New York, 1985, p. 155.

[37]*Ibid.*

[38]*Ibid.,* p. 157.

[39]Douglas A. Boyd and Joseph D. Straubhaar, "Developmental Impact of the Home Video Cassette Recorder on Third World Countries," *Journal of Broadcasting & Electronic Media,* Volume 29, Number 1, Winter 1985, p. 7. (From Marshall McLuhan's *The Medium is the Message,* p. 131.)

[40]Oswald H. Ganley and Gladys D. Ganley, *To Inform Or to Control? The New Communications Network.* McGraw-Hill, New York, 1982, p. 123.

[41]John Miller, "The Latest Threat to Soviet Society," *The Boston Globe,* November 8, 1982, p. 1. (Reprinted from the *London Telegraph*).

[42]*Ibid.*

[43]Alison Smale, "Soviets Battle Black Market in Western Movie Cassettes," *The Philadelphia Inquirer,* April 10, 1983, p. I-5.

[44]Ned Temko, "Kremlin Sees Threat in Uncensored Videocassettes," *The Christian Science Monitor,* May 12, 1983, p. 2.

[45]*Ibid.*

[46]Loren Graham, *Computers in the Soviet Union,* Program on Information Resources Policy Seminar, Harvard, February 4, 1985.

[47]Donald R. Shanor, *Behind the Lines.* See the entire chapter, "The Borscht Pot Antenna," pp. 148–172, for discussions of this and related problems.

[48]Alison Smale, "Soviets Battle Black Market in Western Movie Cassettes," *The Philadelphia Inquirer,* April 10, 1983, p. I-5.

[49]Najwa Kefay, "Jordan. Not Enough Films," *InterMedia,* July/September 1983, p. 60.

[50]Jerzy Pomorski, "Poland. Waiting for Video," *InterMedia,* July/September 1983, p. 66.

[51]"Polish Strike is Shown in Warsaw," *The New York Times,* January 13, 1981, p. A-10.

[52]*Ibid.*

[53]Jerzy Pomorski, "Poland. Waiting for Video," *InterMedia,* July/September 1983, p. 66.

[54]*Ibid.*

[55]Bogdan Turek, "High-Ranking Polish Official Sentenced," *United Press International,* January 14, 1984 (NEXIS).

[56]*Ibid.*

[57]*Ibid.*

[58]*Ibid.*

[59]Bradley Graham, "Polish Resistance Flourishes Under Eyes of Regime," *The Washington Post,* November 26, 1983, p. A-1.

See also:

Steven Erlanger, "Poland. A Nation in Turmoil, A Populace in Despair," *The Boston Globe,* March 27, 1985, p. 1, which mentions videocassettes as among the items included in "the immense outpouring of underground Solidarity literature" in the mid-1980s.

[60]Teresa Hanicka, "Underground Video Tape Production," Situation Report, Poland/8, *Radio Free Europe Research,* Radio Free Europe-Radio Liberty, May 21, 1985, p. 23.

[61]*Ibid.* See also p. 24, and:

"In the World of Independent Culture"; "Fewer Setbacks, More Books: A Talk With the Independent Publishing House NOWa"; and "NOWa-Video", all in "Extracts From Polish Underground Publications," Teresa Hanicka and Nika Krzeczunowicz, compilers and translators, RAD Polish Underground Extracts/8, *Radio Free Europe Research,* Radio Free Europe-Radio Liberty, May 21, 1985, pp. 3–9, 13–20, and 29, respectively.

[62]"In the World of Independent Culture," in "Extracts From Polish Underground Publications," Teresa Hanicka and Nika Krzeczunowicz, compilers and translators, RAD Polish Underground Extracts/8, *Radio Free Europe Research,* Radio Free Europe-Radio Liberty, May 21, 1985, p. 6.

[63]Elihu Katz, "Israel. A Second TV Channel?", *InterMedia,* July/September, 1983, pp. 55–56.

[64]Lasanda Kurukulasuriya, "The Rich Relax With Imported Video," *InterMedia,* July/September 1983, pp. 68–69.

[65]William K. Stevens, "Bazaars of India Are Now a Toyland of High Tech," *The New York Times,* February 2, 1984, p. A-2.

See also:

T. N. Ninan and Chander Uday Singh, "India's Entertainment Revolution," *World Press Review,* September, 1983, p. 58.

M. A. Partha Sarathy, "India. Video On The Bus," *InterMedia,* July/September 1983, p. 53.

[66]James W. Hatton, "Film Industry Struggling in Bangladesh," *The Associated Press,* April 23, 1981 (NEXIS).

[67]Denis D. Gray, "Blue Jeans and "E.T." Have Crept In, But Burma Remains Isolated," *The Associated Press,* January 27, 1983 (NEXIS).

[68]Colin Campbell, "Rock, B-Movies and Traffic Tie-Ups are Making Inroads on Burmese Life," *The New York Times,* July 23, 1983, p. A-2.

[69]*Ibid.*

[70]Christopher S. Wren, "Off-Key Or Off-Color, Tunes of West Worry China," *The New York Times,* October 28, 1982, p. A-2.

[71]Christopher S. Wren, "TV (And With It The World) Comes to Mongolians," *The New York Times,* November 14, 1984, p. A-2.

[72]Pico Iyer, "The Second Revolution. Deng's Reforms are Taking China on a Courageous if Uncharted Course," *Time, September 23, 1985, p. 52.*

[73]*"China Nears Agreement With Western Producers Over Video Copyrights," Variety,* October 23, 1985, p. 1.

[74]*Ibid.*

[75]*Ibid.*

[76]"Dateline: Beijing," *The Xinhua General Overseas News Service,* December 14, 1985 (NEXIS).
See also:

Pico Iyer, "The Second Revolution. Deng's Reforms are Taking China on a Courageous if Uncharted Course," *Time,* September 23, 1985, pp. 45–46.

[77]"Dateline: Beijing," *The Xinhua General Overseas News Service,* December 14, 1985 (NEXIS).
[78]*Ibid.*

[79]Elihu Katz, "Israel, A Second TV Channel?", *InterMedia,* July/September 1983, p. 56.

[80]" 'Homevid' to Pubs," *Variety,* October 24, 1984, p. 396.

[81]Gholam Hoseyn Sa'edi, "Iran Under the Party of God," *Index on Censorship,* February 1984, p. 16.

South Korea. Personal communications.

[82]George Jahn, "Video Cassette Black Market Flourishes in Hungary," *The Associated Press,* April 26, 1985, (NEXIS).

[83]*Ibid.*

[84]G. S., "Video Wave Hits Bulgaria," Situation Report, Bulgaria/3, *Radio Free Europe Research,* Radio Free Europe-Radio Liberty, February 1984, p. 5.

[85]*Ibid.*

[86]*Ibid.*

[87]*Ibid.*

[88]"Paris," *Variety, August 22, 1984, p. 135.*

[89]*"U.K.'s Vid Express," Variety,* November 9, 1984, p. 47.

[90]M. A. Partha Sarathy, "India. Video On The Bus," *InterMedia,* July/September 1983, p. 53.

[91]"Catching A Bus," *Variety,* August 15, 1984, p. 43.

[92]"Early Warning. Media Beat," *World Press Review,* August 1984, p. 6.

[93]*Ibid.*

[94]"Ships Fitted with Video Tape Recorders," *BBC Summary of World Broadcasting,"* February 19, 1983 (NEXIS).

See also:

Video Copyright Action Against Shipping Line," *BBC Summary of World Broadcasting,* October 24, 1983 (NEXIS).

[95]Tess Thomas, "Jamaica. The Miami Connection," *InterMedia,* July/September 1983, p. 57.

[96]"Scratch, Look, Listen," *Observer,* 8 April 1984, p. 23.

[97]*Ibid.*

[98]*Ibid.*

CHAPTER EIGHT

Expressed Concerns by Governments Regarding VCRs and Videocassettes

Throughout the research for this study, the mildness of *overtly expressed* concerns by governments over VCR and cassette proliferation has been striking.* With the exception of Iran, some major communist countries, and Malaysia and Indonesia, governments have mostly indicated general frustration and rather minor perceived threats. In several instances, VCRs have been banned or are grumbled about for ostensibly economic, not political, reasons.

In Iran, in an effort to "purify" the universities, many of the textbooks have been rewritten, professors have been fired, and students who have been " 'polluted' by Western ideas"[1] are not allowed to attend classes. American and Western programming is banned on television and in the cinemas, and Muzak has been removed from hotel lobbies.[2] But such material floats freely on videocassettes through the black market and is avidly sought by the owners of banned videocassette recorders.[3] The Islamic government of Iran is sufficiently concerned to exact heavy penalties, even death sentences, for videocassette possession and selling.[4] Such severe punishment has not been discovered during this study for any other Muslim, or indeed, any other, country. The rise in the influence of the Arab oil-exporting nations, and, more especially, the Iranian revolution, have made an enormous impression on Muslims in numerous nations. Indeed, the one major political topic that has been seen constantly in combination with the spread of VCRs and videocassettes is the tug of war between the more forward-looking and the more fundamentalist Muslims. All Muslim eyes seem turned toward Iran: those of the moderates from fear that the Iranian revolution might be exported, and those of the fundamentalists from a desire for emulation. Muslims are among the most avid seekers after VCRs and videocassettes that have been discovered. This is interesting because of rising Muslim unrest and political participation. Professor James Bill, an Islami specialist at the University of Texas, has been quoted as saying, " 'Over the next 40 years . . . populist Islam is going to be the most important ideological force in the world'."[5] The Islamic faith is practiced by a fifth of the world's people, and "The House of Islam" is made up of 67 nations.[6] Several overt political acts

---

* It could well be that this aspect has been overlooked in reporting.

have been committed with videocassettes by Muslims (see Chapter 9). It is also interesting that, while the print medium may still be the predominant carrier of political messages in the largely literate communist world, audio and videocassettes are emerging as the main political conduits of the largely illiterate Muslims.

Saudi Arabia, which finds itself in the curious position of being the most conservative of all Muslim societies, but at the same time of having to protect itself against the Shiite brand of fundamentalism, has cracked down somewhat on videocassette circulation. So far as can be seen, this is not because of fundamentalist content, but for content that could offend internal conservative factions and thus weaken the control of the Saudi government. An American, Alvin Levine, was arrested, for instance, and charged with distributing pornographic videotapes.[7] Levine was conducting a videotape trading club for Americans inside the Aramco compound. Saudi law enforcement in general has become more rigid as the Islamic regimes in the Persian Gulf—Iran and Iraq—have become more threatening.[8]

In Malaysia, the moderate Islamic government is having to walk a religious tightrope. It wants to bring Malaysian viewers back to broadcast television, from which they have defected in droves to videocassette programming. It has partly accomplished this by permitting a new private video channel, TV3, offering: "western soap operas, variety shows, Hong Kong movies and exclusive Olympic coverage . . . "[9] This has been so popular that

> residents in Malacca, 100 miles away [from Kuala Lumpur], have rigged pots and pans to their television aeriels to pick up the station.[10]*

Fundamentalist Malaysian Muslims are not happy, however, and are demanding that the new channel, like the old ones, carry Malay religious programs. Except for adding some traditional music, there has been no compliance. *The Economist* remarks,

> if the new channel carried more religious programmes, viewers would simply return to watching videos. Some 45% of television owners around Kuala Lumpur also have a video cassette recorder, one of the highest rates in the world. Almost half of them are ethnic Chinese, but it was also found that 38% of Malay viewers, who are Moslems by definition, watched videotapes during religious programmes.[12]

---

* Donald Shanor projects an information future for Russia in which satellite broadcasts from Japan or Europe "could be picked up by home hobby shop equipment, perhaps with a dish antenna made from borscht pots or other scrap metal, and taped for use on home videocassette players."[11]

The contest between the traditional and the modern Muslims in Malaysia has produced one of the most interesting examples of what VCRs could portend politically. In fall 1984, challenged by Prime Minister Dutak Seri Mahathir Mohamad, three leading member of his governing United Malays National Organization (UMNO) were scheduled to debate three members of the small minority fundamentalist Pan-Malaysian Islamic Party (PAS) on television.[13] The subject of the two-hour debate was to be "kafir-mengkafir," or "the trading of accusations that others are non-believers . . . "[14] PAS had been telling its members, "mainly unsophisticated Malay villagers in Malaysia's predominantly Malay northern penisular states,"[15] that members of UMNO were non-believers. The PAS members were therefore refusing to pay taxes or to use government-owned cemeteries. The prime minister hoped the debate would make PAS "prove" its charges, but most people felt it could only be disasterous. At the eleventh hour, the Malaysian king and the ruling sultans halted the debate, to the great relief of Malaysians and their neighbors. For, among Malaysia's neighbors,* there were some who had

> expressed specific concern about the unsettling effect that . . . a videotaped and widely circulated TV debate [on such a volatile issue] could have on their own domestic situations . . . [18]

Two similar situations have occurred, in which neighbors not only worried about but protested the television of others, partly for fear of videocassette dispersal. In 1980, Saudi Arabia exerted international pressure to stop the showing of the British/U.S. docudrama "Death of a Princess" in a large number of countries.[19] In 1984, the Indian Foreign Minister reprimanded the U.S. Ambassador and the British High Commissioner for their respective countries' TV coverage of the aftermath of Indira Gandhi's assassination.[20] In the first instance, videocassettes of the protested documentary were smuggled to the people of Saudi Arabia within 24 hours after it was

---

* Indonesia, for instance, is 90% Muslim, with 153 million people of that religion.[16] Indonesia has also been having major trouble with its more fundamentalist Muslims, or those outside the government who use Islam as a political weapon. *The New York Times,* discussing September 1984 rioting, said: "A large issue was the Government's plan to enforce 'Pancasila' as the sole state ideology."[17] The doctrine was announced by the founders of Indonesia when they declared independence from the Netherlands in 1945, and written into Indonesia's constitution. The ideology espouses "belief in one supreme God, just and civilized humanity, nationalism, democracy, and social justice," and was intended to make the government secular. Pancasila and Islam coexisted until about two years ago, when Suharto announced that all "sociopolitical groups" must adopt it. This has been interpreted to mean that it may interfere with Islam, and has offered an excellent opening for Suharto's opposition. While most propaganda is said to have been confined to pamphleteering, Malaysia did ban Indonesian audiocassettes that were politically oriented.

aired in Great Britain. It is highly probably that videocassettes were also made and distributed of both the objectionable scenes shown by British television and of "American television pictures showing Sikhs rejoicing and drinking champagne after Mrs. Gandhi's assassination."[21]

In Indonesia, the government is said to be "definitely concerned about the VTR explosion, and especially about the underground black market in uncensored tapes. . . ."[22] But, although the government has effectively nationalized the videocassette industry (see Chapter 10) and is attempting to control the video black market,

> many elite audiences are quite matter-of-fact about the "door-to-door" video rental salesmen who arrive on a motorcycle with a black briefcase full of 50–75 titles, mostly abysmal in quality of reproduction — but of popular and relatively new films.[23]

United Press International adds an important dimension to the above statements by saying,

> Indonesian authorities also are concerned over the proliferation of videotapes with political content or martial arts productions subtitled in Chinese — both regarded as subversive.[24]

After an attempted coup in 1965, Indonesia broke diplomatic relations with China and forbade the use of Chinese characters. Indonesia has recently been attempting to play an expanding role both regionally and globally, and *The Christian Science Monitor* says that it has a number of reasons for its "Chinese obsession." Locally, the Chinese in Indonesia are resented for their economic power. They often suffer from discrimination, although this is against official policy. The Indonesians are suspicious of the loyalty of its 4 million Chinese citizens to the point that

> all Chinese script in magazines and newspapers entering the country is blacked out for fear that it might contain secret and inflammatory messages from Peking.
>
> In regional terms, Indonesia perceives China's sheer size and its increasing economic power as future destabilizing factors in the region. The chief of Indonesia's Armed Forces, Gen. Benny Murdani, recently told foreign reporters that as China progresses, it will be capable of causing harm to the economies of Indonesia and other Southeast Asian nations.[25]

Indonesia is disturbed about all the attention being given to China by the West and the United States especially. Says Indonesia's Foreign Minister Mochtar Kusumaatmadja:

"We feel they lavish too much attention on China and don't pay enough to the fast-growing, dynamic countries of southeast Asia . . . All this worries us; the Chinese are too smart. . . ."[26]

While the Indonesians may be paranoid about China, this study has revealed multi-faceted factors in China that bear watching:

1. China is the only communist country so far identified in this study that is producing and vigorously exporting videocassettes, along with other beefed-up exports. In fall 1984, through Solid Video of Hong Kong, China was said to be "aggressively involved in the international video industry,"[27] offering a list of 60 titles. Of these, "Though family-type programs and costume dramas predominate . . . there are some martial arts subjects featuring Li Lianjie, a highly popular exponent of the art."[28] The sound tracks of these features were produced in Mandarin but are being dubbed into Cantonese, understandable to most overseas Chinese, and into English.

2. China has recently revived its film industry, producing 127 films in 1983, up from 20 in 1977. Many of these films are already in the export market. Although the themes permitted have been relaxed a great deal, no Chinese films are totally devoid of political content.[29]

3. China is appealing strongly — and in many cases, successfully — to its overseas sons (however long gone). It is asking them to bring money home to China, to help rebuild their "motherland." It is said to be a rare Chinese who is not somewhat afflicted with a perhaps unrealistic but nevertheless real "homesickness."* As the *Far Eastern Economic Review* puts it:

> what is this pervasive tie to the Chinese motherland, this tenacious insistance, from Sydney to Amsterdam, on Chineseness? Is it a question of race, culture, politics, family or ancestors? It is, by all accounts, a mixture of all these things. Some Overseas Chinese get quite misty-eyed about it, such as an Indonesian writing in a Hongkong magazine: "Back in my southern hemisphere, I feel the wind of the night in my face and lean out of my window, looking longingly at the stars — I pray with all my heart for the glory and good fortune of my ancestral land."[30]

It quotes a Chinese American who said in a Hong Kong magazine:

> " 'China' is a cultural entity which flows incessantly, like the Yellow River, from its source all the way to the present time, and from here to a boundless future. This is the basic and unshakeable belief in the mind of every Chinese.

---

* One must be careful, of course, not to succumb to the "once a Chinese, always a Chinese" syndrome.

It is also the strongest basis for Chinese nationalism. No matter which government is in power, people will not reject China, for there is always hope for a better future a hundred or more years from now."[31]

4. The government of China is highly enthusiastic about what VCRs can be used for institutionally, and praises them for everything from promoting panda welfare to reinforcing the belief of youth in the benefits of both communism and the "responsibility" program.[32]

5. China is deeply concerned by the influx of VCRs and videocassettes and other materials which has resulted in large part from its "open door" policy. This concern led to a brief but vigorous campaign to stamp out "spiritual pollution" in fall 1983. However, "spiritual pollution" was quickly seized on by the opposition to condemn all liberalization, including economic changes. After only two months, the campaign was sacrificed to save what was obviously considered a program of higher priority: China's bid for modernization.[33]

This may be a series of coincidental happenings and they may go nowhere. But the speed and determination with which China has been turning around both its economic system and its lifestyle, and its obvious recognition of the videocassette's power, would indicate a strong potential for political happenings from this series of events in the future.

India is said to "keep an eye" on what is circulated, because it doesn't want things shown that might upset its neighbors.[34] Although the entire bustling Indian video business is illegal, the government appears to largely ignore it.[35] The Secretary to the Indian government's Ministry of Information and Broadcasting is said to be disdainful of VCRs which permit Indians to see shows like "Dallas," for cultural reasons not allowed on Indian television.[36] Israel, which is in deep economic trouble, put a ban on VCRs and other luxury imports in fall 1984. Otherwise, the Israeli government concerns itself only if a videocassette is seen as "damaging to the security of the state," overlooking pornography, although it is illegal. The government of South Korea forbids pornography to be shown in public places like coffee shops, and punishes offenders. The government of Pakistan is mainly concerned with banned Indian films and porno, although it *has* required that VCRs be licensed.[37]

In Thailand, there is

discussion in the media of the long term effect of the heavy exposure of foreign culture. TV has been used as a carefully controlled "unifier" and purveyor of Thai culture. The VCR counteracts this influence.[38]

Many countries that are trying to maintain traditional cultures feel they are losing the battle in part due to VCRs, for their citizens are avidly obtaining and watching fare this way that is otherwise forbidden. In 1983, *Reuters* surveyed 15 Asian countries: Pakistan, Malaysia, Indonesia, Bangladesh, Taiwan, Burma, India, Sri Lanka, Thailand, the Philippines, South Korea, China, Japan, Hong Kong, and Singapore.[39] Only Japan — which has the most to gain from VCR as well as blank tape sales — was found to have no VCR-inspired cultural or other worries.* The other governments were said to be mainly concerned with the crime, violence, and explicit sex shown in the available videocassette programming, although "films with racial and religious overtones or a tinge of Communism do not pass the censors in many nations."[40] Most cassettes never get near a censor, however. In most of these countries, extremely high percentages (in some, practically all) of the videocassettes are both pirated and smuggled.

Segun Olusola, the managing director of the Nigerian Television Authority, expressed the general frustration of governments that would like to continue to exercise control over audiovisual programming when he called VCRs the "enemy in our backyards,"[41] and a discussion of them in the context of Nigeria's War Against Indiscipline "like a reconnaissance trip into enemy territory. . . ." Mr. Olusola says "video recorders and their message must be discussed because they have become a world phenomenon like missiles or the war heads they carry or drugs."[42]

The Nigerian military government which took power in a late 1983 coup, and has been itself replaced, sought weapons for what it called a War Against Indiscipline. It turned immediately to radio and television, Mr. Olusola says. But

> when television is used as a weapon of War — it becomes the exhorter, the guide, the teacher and leader and the constant reminder of the dangers of backsliding. And it cannot even begin to attempt any of those things if it is not being watched.[45]

Alas, the Nigerians, he says, have tuned out broadcast television and are instead watching videocassettes. He is quite sarcastic about what worthless things they are watching using the VCR:

> Religious crusades and cure-me-quick sessions of the most extreme sort.

> The regular blue-films containing explicit front view scenes of sexual debauchery and deviations.

> Direct exhortations and introduction to the mechanics of the elimination of opponents. [Political films, apparently].

---

* Japan mainly sells, not leases, videocassettes, which helps to cut down a bit on what is in circulation. Rentals are gaining, however.

Festivals of disco and drugs — unlimited.

All other cultural manifestations of the second generation European civilisation of the fringe.[44]

Olusola says that Nigerian authorities expect television to support social values, to educate the people, to teach them self-discipline, to "disseminate impartially and objectively news and opinions," and to "promote . . . physical, mental and social well-being. . . ."[45] To achieve the objectives, Olusola says that videocassettes "should be harnessed and guided."[46] He intimates that this could be done through the right kind of videocassette programming, but does not say how he will get the people to watch it.

Boyd and Straubhaar have remarked on the frustration of development plans of governments by the advent of VCRs, saying that "VCRs, in fact, may undermine the development process because of the nature of programming used by owners."[47] They mention Saudi Arabia as a specific example. The Saudis, they say, are not only watching what they choose to on VCRs, but they have simply stopped watching governmental messages on television.[48] The same thing, they say, applies to Egypt, where the villagers who used to cluster around to watch broadcast TV now cluster around to watch videocassette programming:

The Arab culture generally dictates that radio and television receivers are shared with extended families and friends . . . In many of these Egyptian villages, therefore, the VCR has replaced or heavily supplemented viewing of the state-run television system. Because of this, development-oriented programs intended for villagers are often not seen by the target audience . . . [49]

The Indian Secretary of the Ministry of Information and Broadcasting gives that country's television philosophy:

"In a developed country, TV is primarily a vehicle of entertainment. But in a developing country you have to contend with old perceptions and sometimes medieval prejudices . . . our programs have to be socially relevant. We treat information . . . as an extension agency of the government to bring about social change . . . to fight against the superstitions . . . which hamper progress toward a modern scientific industrial society . . . So, the important agenda of our programming is modern agriculture, problems of women and children, family welfare, uplift of the poor, adult education, rural development, social welfare, labor problems. . . ."[50]

But this informational and educational programming is not on the "most watched" list of Indian audiences. "Most watched" are Hindi films, a program of film songs, serials (mainly Western), and news programs. Indian

TV was expanded in 1985 to reach 70% of the population. Only 23% had previously been able to tune in.[51]

By far the most frequent and loudly expressed concerns about VCRs and videocassettes have to do with pornography, and with sex and violence in programming. Especially when VCRs are first introduced into a country, pornography is incredibly popular. Interest tends to pall somewhat — or becomes diluted — as more varied programming becomes available. The interest of viewers, and objections of governments, remain strongest in the most traditional cultures and restricted societies. It should, however, be noted that some of the professed moral outrage may have much deeper political significance. Such concerns have long been the blanket excuse for censorship which is much more encompassing. The governments of the Soviet Union and Eastern Europe, for instance, make a lot of noise about pornography. But it is "political pornography" (actually called that by the Russians) that is the central issue.[52]

Many of the most vocal protests come from the democracies. A majority of Australian states voted to outlaw X-rated videos because of community pressures concerning "violent and degrading pornography. . . ."[53] This vote, says *Variety*, "will simply mean they are sold under the counter in sex video shops or by mail order. . . ."[54]

The British attempted to rush through a Video Recordings Bill in summer 1984 in an effort to control what they call "video nasties."[55] *The Economist* at that time said that this bill was inspired by "some widely-publicised bogus research"[56] which claimed to show that nearly half of all British school children had seen such videos as "I Spit on Your Grave," "Zombie Flesh Eaters," "The Evil Dead," and "Driller Killer," which variously feature decapitation, dismemberment, and cannibalism.* "Research" by British journalists showed that the same children just as happily confessed to having seen non-existent titles. But, says *The Economist,* this did not keep the opponents of the bill from being "shouted down as a defense of perversion. . . ."[57] *Variety reported in October 1985 that*

> last month the Video Recordings Act became law in Britain, virtually enabling the state to decide what films citizens may watch in the privacy of their homes for the first time in history.[58]

Despite passage of this Act, the Parliamentary Group Video Inquiry, "an influential British lobby of politicians and churchmen," released a report the same month entitled "Video Violence and Children," demanding "A review of existing law, and . . . additional legislation."[59] The British Videogram

---

* These are also known as "slashers" and "snuff" movies, since lots of people get slashed up and snuffed out.

Association was reported as calling this " 'overkill,' " saying that "police actions under the Obscene Publications Act and the new homevid classification laws" had " 'effectively dealt with the problem.' "[60]

In Canada, where the border with the U.S. is described as a "sieve," pornography is on a long list of forbidden items.[61] But it comes in in large quantities, lots of it now on videocassettes, and is widely duplicated and distributed. In 1982, fed up with the child porn, violent sex, and bestiality said to be featured in videocassettes rented by a chain of 13 Red Hot Video outlets, a women's group set fire to two of them.[62] Credit for the burnings was claimed by a "radical feminist" group called Wimmin's* Fire Brigade. *Maclean's* says

> the B.C. [British Columbia] Federation of Women, representing a wide political spectrum of 36 groups in the province, stopped short of condoning the arson but it was clearly sympathetic. . . .[63]

Given the enormous amount of American programming (both legal and illegal) making the VCR rounds, this study has found extremely little anti-American commentary regarding VCRs.** Major exceptions are seen in Iran, the USSR, and Eastern Europe. But most countries are used to seeing a lot of American programming on TV and in the movies, and the wider variety available on videocassettes seems to be regarded as just an extension.

Private citizens everywhere are seen to take a special delight in having short-circuited, via piracy and smuggling, the usual long wait for American and other films and TV programming. There is a not quite expressed sense that many governments, especially in the less affluent parts of the world, share in the joy of attaining this status. Although it is not usually said in so many words, governments, in some cases, appear relieved to have entertainment for their people without having to put forth the money to provide it. Christine Ogan, of the Indiana University School of Journalism, has expressed this, saying:

> why do countries permit virtually unrestricted use of video when it frequently violates existing communication policies? One reason is that it takes the heat off governments without means or inclination to improve existing broadcast programmes. . . .[65]

---

* This spelling was adopted because of this group's aversion to "men."

** There is no lack of anti-American feeling in the world, as can be attested to by an article in the fall 1984 issue of *Orbis.*[64] Seeming lack of concern may simply represent lack of available information. That 90% of VCRs are Japanese could also be diverting anti-Western animosity. Further, countries may hesitate to make a big fuss about VCR programming unless they are prepared to do something about it.

This could account, at least in part, for their "benign neglect" of what might otherwise be seen as a major problem.

Several of the author's personal contacts commented that VCRs, whether obtained legally or illegally, were freely available in the country of their knowledge, that the government did not seem to be worried, and that the videocassette business, however irregular in nature, was, in fact, regarded as a sort of "growth industry."[66]

Governments may also be cashing in. *Variety* reports:

The Indonesian government is under attack from the world record industry for permitting a claimed 30,000,000 pirate cassettes to be exported each year. Per the Intl. Federation of Phonogram and Videogram Producers (IFPI), the Indonesian government has earned $300,000 alone from official taxes on bootlegs of this year's Live Aid famine relief concerts. . . .[67]

Variety has also reported the arrest of an Indonesian businessman in Manhattan for selling pirated audiocassettes, with the aid of New York's Indonesian consulate, to Recording Industry Association of America (RIAA) undercover operatives.[68]

NOTES

[1]Chris Kutschera, "Inside Iran," *The Middle East,* December 1984, p. 25.

[2]"Iran. Five Years of Fanaticism," *The New York Times Magazine,* February 12, 1984, pp. 21 ff.

[3]Ray Vicker, "Dubai's Traders are Building a Thriving Trade Smuggling Goods Into Iran," *The Wall Street Journal,* May 7, 1980, p. 48. Reprinted as "Dubai's Enterprising Traders Smuggle Goods Into Iran," in Burgess Laughlin, *Black Markets Around the World,* Loompanics, Unlimited, Mason, MI, 1981, pp. 35–37.

[4]"Censorship and Entertainment in Iran," United States Information Agency (USIA) unclassified cable, U.S. Department of State from the U.S. Mission, Berlin, September 1985.

[5]Kenneth Woodward, Elizabeth O. Colton, Melinda Liu, Jane Whitmore, "Islam Versus The West," *Newsweek,* June 24, 1985, p. 28.

[6]*Ibid.*

[7]Jim Anderson, "Saudi-Americans," *United Press International,* October 18, 1983 (NEXIS).

[8]*Ibid.,* and also:

"Relative Jailed in Saudi Arabia Threatens Suicide," *The Associated Press,* October 19, 1983 (NEXIS).

[9]"Malaysian Television. Clearing the Air," *The Economist,* September 8, 1984, p. 96.

[10]*Ibid.*

[11]Donald R. Shanor, *Behind The Lines. The Private War Against Soviet Censorship.* St. Martin's Press, New York, 1985, p. 149.

[12]"Malaysian Television. Clearing The Air," *The Economist,* September 8, 1984, p. 96.

For modernity vs. fundamentalism in Malaysia, see:

Tom Ashbrook, "Modern Malaysia 'Shooting for the Moon.' Prosperity at Hand, but Religious, Racial Divisions Remain," *The Boston Globe,* December 10, 1984, p. 2.

Michael Specter, "The 'Small Town' Big City," *Far Eastern Economic Review,* September 27, 1984, pp. 23–25.

V. S. Naipaul, "Conversations in Malaysia: The Primitive Faith," *Among the Believers. An Islamic Journey,* Vintage Books, New York, 1982, pp. 225–296.

[13]"Islam on the Screen," *The Economist,* October 27, 1984, p. 45.

[14]James Clad, "They Shall Not Pas. Umno Challenges the Opposition Over Who Is More Islamic Than Whom," *Far Eastern Economic Review,* October 18, 1984, p. 16.

[15]Rodney Tasker, "The Great Non-Debate," *Far Eastern Economic Review,* November 22, 1984, p. 30.

[16]Kenneth L. Woodward, Elizabeth O. Colton, Melinda Liu and June Whitmore, "Islam Versus The West, *Newsweek,* June 24, 1985, p. 28.

[17]"Jakarta Violence Laid to Militants," *The New York Times,* September 16, 1984, p. A-11.

[18]James Clad, "They Shall Not Pas. Umno Challenges the Opposition Over Who Is More Islamic Than Whom," *Far Eastern Economic Review,* October 18, 1984, p. 16.

[19]Thomas White and Gladys D. Ganley, *The 'Death of A Princess' Controversy,* Program on Information Resources Policy, Harvard University, 1983.

[20]"India Protests U.S. TV Coverage," *The New York Times,* November 9, 1984, p. A-8.

[21]*Ibid.*

[22]Indonesia. Personal communications.

The 118-page regulations regarding videocassettes are called *Presidential Decision Number 13 for the Year 1983. Decision of the Minister of Information of the Republic of Indonesia Concerning Video Cassette Recordings.* They were signed by President Suharto on February 26, 1983.

[23]Indonesia. Personal communications.

[24]Isabelle Reckeweg, "Jakarta, Indonesia," *United Press International,* April 26, 1983 (NEXIS).

[25]Kieran Cooke, "Jakarta's Shadow Stretches Farther Across Asian Politics," *The Christian Science Monitor,* January 21, 1985, p. 9.

[26]*Ibid.*

[27]"China Exports Video Via Hong Kong Firm," *Variety,* October 10, 1984, p. 38.

[28]*Ibid.*

[29]Ambrose Eichenberger, "Cinema After Mao," *World Press Review,* January 1983, p. 61.

"Chinese Cinema. Shadows From the Past," *The Economist,* January 5, 1985, pp. 73–74.

Mark I. Pinsky, "A Small Leap Forward," *American Film,* April 1984, pp. 52–54.

Li Wenbin, "China's New Realism," *World Press Review,* August 1984, p. 59.

"China To Build $70M 'Film City'," *The Boston Globe,* February 1, 1985, p. 30.

[30]Ian Buruma, "Call of the Motherland," *Far Eastern Economic Review,* November 22, 1984, p. 46.

[31]*Ibid.*

[32]"Growing Number of Chinese College Students Believe in Marxism," *The Xinhua General Overseas News Service,* December 27, 1982 (NEXIS).

Paul Loong, "Chinese Try to Rescue Ancient Music," *United Press International,* July 4, 1982 (NEXIS).

" 'Love for Panda' Show in Beijing," *The Xinhua General Overseas News Service,* July 14, 1984 (NEXIS).

[33]Liang Heng and Judith Shapiro, "Chinese Contradictions," *Index on Censorship,* December 1984, pp. 6, 32.

Liang Heng and Judith Shapiro, *Intellectual Freedom in China After Mao.* Fund for Free Expression Report, New York, 1984.

"Smuggling," *Reuters,* November 29, 1983 (NEXIS).

Three dispatches called "Pornography," *Reuters,* March 4, 1982; September 9, 1982; and January 6, 1983 (NEXIS).

[34]India. Personal communications.

[35]T. N. Ninan and Chander Uday Singh, "India's Entertainment Revolution," *World Press Review*, September 1983, p. 58, among others.

[36]Arthur Unger, "TV Comes to India: A Talk With Its Top Broadcast Official," *The Christian Science Monitor*, March 22, 1985, p. 25.

[37]Israel, South Korea, and Pakistan. Personal communications.

[38]Thailand. Personal communications.

[39]Francis Daniel, "Dateline: Singapore," *Reuters*, September 20, 1983 (NEXIS).

[40]*Ibid.*

[41]Segun Olusola, *Giving Video a Second Chance in Nigeria*, Speech, International Institute of Communications 1984 Annual Conference, Berlin, September 22, 1984, p. 1.

[42]*Ibid.*, p. 2.

[43]*Ibid.*, p. 3.

[44]*Ibid.*, pp. 3-4.

[45]*Ibid.*, p. 5.

[46]*Ibid.*, p. 6.

[47]Douglas A. Boyd and Joseph D. Straubhaar, "Developmental Impact of the Home Video Cassette Recorder on Third World Countries," *Journal of Broadcasting & Electronic Media*, Volume 29, Number 1, Winter 1985, p. 9.

[48]*Ibid.*, p. 11.

[49]*Ibid.*, p. 12.

[50]Arthur Unger, "TV Comes to India: A Talk With Its Top Broadcast Official," *The Christian Science Monitor*, March 22, 1985, p. 25.

[51]*Ibid.*

[52]The Soviet Union. Personal communications.

[53]"Oz Lawmakers Mull New Ratings for Non-Violent Erotic Vidtapes," *Variety*, November 9, 1984, p. 50.

[54]Don Groves, "X-Rated Backlash Building in Oz; Govt. Officials Start to Backpedal," *Variety*, September 12, 1984, p. 37.

[55]" 'Big Brother' Busy Classifying Titles; Use More Checkers," *Variety*, January 16, 1985, p. 109.

[56]"The Home Movie Censor" *The Economist*, October 20, 1984, p. 62.

[57]*Ibid.*

[58]"British Report Calls For More Vid Legislation," *Variety*, October 23, 1985, p. 1.

[59]*Ibid.*

[60]*Ibid.*

[61]Malcolm Gray, "No Sex, Please, We're Victorian," *Maclean's*, July 5, 1982, p. 15.

[62]Malcolm Gray, "The Ladies Are For Burning," *Maclean's*, December 6, 1982, p. 21.

[63]*Ibid.*

[64]Alvin Z. Rubenstein and Donald B. Smith, "Anti-Americanism In The Third World," *Orbis*, Vol. 28, No. 3, Fall, 1984, pp. 593-614. Reprinted in *Current News*, U.S. Air Force, U.S. Department of Defense, January 23, 1985, pp. 1-12.

[65]Christine L. Ogan, "Media Diversity and Communications Policy. Impact of VCRs and Satellite TV," *Telecommunications Policy*, March 1985, p. 66.

[66]See Appendix A.

Boyd and Straubhaar also mention the "Cottage Industry" aspect of Third World underground videocassette copying and distribution. Douglas A. Boyd and Joseph D. Straubhaar, "Developmental Impact of The Home Video Cassette Recorder on Third World Countries," *Journal of Broadcasting & Electronic Media*, Volume 29, No. 1, Winter 1985, p. 10.

Comments have frequently been seen and heard that the videocassette business is the one booming area in an otherwise sluggish economy in many countries.

[67]"Indonesian Govt. Under Attack For Allowing 'Live Aid' Piracy," *Variety,* December 11, 1985, p. 132.

[68]Ken Terry, "Alleged Indonesian Tape Pirate Arrested With Help of RIAA; Consular Attache Implicated," *Variety,* January 29, 1986, p. 77.

CHAPTER NINE

Varieties of Global Political Acts Involving VCRs and Videocassettes

Quite a wide variety of overt political uses have been made of VCRs and videocassettes, both by citizens and by governments. The following is a description of some of them.

While, of course, closely related to acts perpetrated through film, television, radio and print technology, and following in the footsteps of audiocassettes, these VCR-related acts give a sense of new and expanded political opportunities. Many of the acts work in tandem with or in support of other media. The ingenuity of uses and of some combinations of uses points toward an increase in such activities in the future.

VIDEO TO CIRCUMVENT CONTROLLED MEDIA IN TIMES OF POLITICAL CRISIS

Nora Quebral, chairman of the Department of Development Communication at the University of the Philippines at Los Banos, said in a 1984 speech in Berlin:

> In the weeks after the death of Benigno Aquino, the political figure who was gunned down at the Manila International Airport upon arrival in his home country, one of the hottest items in the video rental shops in the university town where I live was a spliced-up tape of events at the airport and at the funeral which were only very sparingly reported in the mass media at the time. And so I suppose the videocassette recorder could be potentially used to foment revolution . . . in politically unstable countries, just as audio cassettes are said to have helped bring down the last Shah of Iran.[1]

Three weeks after Benigno Aquino's assassination on August 21, 1983, *The New York Times* ran an article saying:

> A customs examiner at Manila International Airport, going through the baggage of a Filipino arriving from Tokyo, ignored a videotape cassette labeled "Playboy Lovers," as the passenger had expected he would.

Later the tape would be viewed in Philippine living rooms for its political interest, since most of the movie had been erased and replaced by a taped copy of a
Japanese documentary on the assassination of Benigno S. Aquino Jr. . . .[2]

This videocassette was said to be just one of many smuggled in from the
U.S. and Japan in the early days after the assassination, and copied and re-
copied on home videocassette recorders for distribution. The cassettes were
mainly made up of sections of American and Japanese network newscasts, or
special treatments by these broadcasters of the subject. Some of the cassettes
were edited to make fairly coherent "documentaries":

One tape producer pieced together excerpts from broadcasts by four networks,
two in Japan and two in the United States, focusing on the unexplained aspects
of the Aquino killing.

Another producer combined sequences from a documentary made by Nihon
Hoso Kyokai, the Japanese Government-supported broadcasting group, and
the privately operated Japanese News Network, and had a Japanese-speaking
friend translate the commentaries into English. With this material he turned
out an English script that can be read along with the action on the screen, and
he made multiple copies for distribution.[3]*

Five months later, it was reported that a group of Filipinos in the U.S.,
called The Ninoy Aquino Movement, had organized a program immediately following Aquino's death under which about 5000 people had sent "at
least two million clippings"[5] of newspaper articles to the Philippines since the
assassination. The group also produced a videocassette, called "Tribute to a
Hero," and sent copies of it to the Philippines. The video included:

Japanese and United States reports on the Philippines as well as speeches by
Senator Edward M. Kennedy . . . Democrat of Massachusetts, and Representative Stephen J. Solarz, Democrat of Brooklyn, who support restoring
constitutional democracy in the Philippines.[6]

In the months following the Aquino assassination, says *The Wall Street
Journal,* "A placid middle class discovered its conscience. . . ."[7] Through

---

* The personal contact for the Philippines did not entirely agree with the description of this
video material as underground. He said: "As to your point about videotapes being smuggled
into the Philippines last year . . . [I] can certainly confirm that there are several versions of
various American and Japanese VTR materials on the . . . tragedy [but] cannot confirm the
New York Times report that some of these tapes were smuggled in 'under the guise of porno.' Excerpts from some of these newscasts or materials recorded at the airport the day of Sen. Aquino's
death have been aired on Philippine television and were shown during the hearings of the
Agrava Fact-Finding Board . . . They certainly are not secret!"[4]

all the above pressures and others, including mass demonstrations, the Philippine people were able to accomplish several things: They got the original investigative commission led by Chief Justice Frenando replaced by a more independent one under Justice Corazon Agrava. They got more balanced news coverage as independent and underground newspapers were allowed to operate. Through rigorous insistence and constant inspection, "One of the nation's freest and fairest elections in recent times was held in May [1984]. . . ."[8]

In October 1984, the investigative commission (albeit with a minority report by the chairperson and a majority report by its members) concluded that, rather than having been gunned down by a hired assassin (Rolando Galman, shot at the scene by Philippine security and charged by the government with the crime), Aquino's murder was the result of a military conspiracy.[9] A number of videotapes as well as audiotapes and still photos played a large part in the commission's conclusions. At the time of the assassination, Aquino was whisked out of the airplane and newsmen and others prevented from following closely enough to get more than fleeting pictures of what then happened. Some weeks later, the German installer revealed that the Manila airport was equipped with a video surveillance system with which to monitor all incoming or outgoing aircraft.[10] When the existence of the system was admitted, it was said to have "unfortunately" only recorded pictures of the tail of Aquino's airplane.[11] But, says *UPI,*

> well-informed sources said the monitoring system, installed as an antihijacking device, is supposed to scan all parts of the airport at any given time. It also has a remote control capability to zoom in on any place and magnify images.[12]

Videos taken by the state-run television and eventually presented to the commission were found to have " 'glitches' resulting from editing."[13] An Indian cinematographer, Subroto Choudhury, asked to analyze the tapes, reported that

> a sequence showing Aquino's China Airlines jet taxiing at the Manila airport was edited. The next shot shows the bullet-riddled bodies of Aquino and Galam lying on the tarmac.[14]

In all, 22 video and audio tape recordings, along with 1430 photographs, were examined by the commission, and many pieced together to refute the government's story. *Newsweek* said:

> General Counsel Andres Narvasa examined some 150 photographs, giving each one a time sequence on the basis of factors such as the amount of blood

under Aquino's head or the progress of a soldier's cap as it tumbles to the ground. Narvasa then matched those pictures with a sound sequence culled from journalists' tapes. . . .[15]

Time reported:

> the Agrava board's legal staff based its argument in large part on the startling discrepancies between shards of evidence, mostly photographs, audio recordings and videotapes . . . and the well-rehearsed military account, recited by a parade of soldiers both on and off the witness stand. . . .[16]

This evidence was said to show that Aquino was shot by someone behind him on the airplane steps, and higher up, instead of, as the military insisted, by an assailant who emerged from under the airplane stairs after Aquino reached the tarmac.[17]

The majority report ended by naming 26 military conspirators, including Constable 1st Class Rogelio Moreno and Sergeant Filomeno Miranda, one of whom is thought to have done the actual killing. It also implicated a number of high-level officers, including — which the chairperson's minority report did not — Chief of Staff General Fabian Ver. General Ver was a longtime advisor and close associate of then President Marcos, and naming him was as close as it was possible to get to holding the Philippine government responsible without actually naming the president.[18]

All of the named conspirators, including General Ver, went to trial, but their aquittal soon became a foregone conclusion. All were, indeed, acquitted on December 2, 1985, the court maintaining that they found " 'all accused innocent of the crimes charged' "[19] rather than that they had been found not guilty. The shooting of Aquino by Galman was maintained, and "the court rejected what it described as 'the much ballyhooed' 150-picture 'photo-chronology' of the events because,"[20] the court insisted,

> it was "without bearing to the issue under discussion" because they involve events after Aquino and Galman were shot. It [the court] also suggested that video tapes and their sound tracks, which recorded both the timing of the shots and voices saying "I'll do it" and "shoot" might possibly have been tampered with.[21]

The court also said

> "there was a strong probability" that *Time* magazine correspondent Sandra Burton, whose audio tape recorded the sounds as Aquino descended the stairs, "was in error" about when she turned it on. . . .[22]

The day following the acquittal of the 26 people accused of killing her husband, Corazon Aquino became the opposition candidate for the Philippine
presidency. After a tumultuous February 1986 election claimed by President
Marcos over strenuous protests, Marcos was forced to flee the Philippines.
How much of the political momentum which led to the installation of Cory
Aquino as the new president can be attributed to videocassettes and
audiocassettes is, of course, debatable, but this technology certainly de-
serves a prominent mention in this incredible political story.

USE OF VIDEOCASSETTES BY SALVADORAN GUERRILLAS*

In August 1984, a *New York Times* article began:

> Ayatollah Ruhollah Khomeini inspired his followers on tape cassettes. The
> Salvadoran guerrillas now promote their cause on Betamax . . . Combining
> the electronic revolution with political revolution, the Salvadoran leftwing
> guerrilla coalition, the Farabundo Marti Front for National Liberation, has
> brought its cause into the plazas of El Salvador with the aid of video cassettes.[25]

The article describes the guerrillas as operating three camera teams that supply an eight-videocassette recorder "network" with propagandistic programming for local uses and make videocassettes available in the U.S. and elsewhere. These

> propaganda films give a highly partial look at the war in El Salvador. It is a war
> where the guerrillas never suffer battlefield defeats, where elections and politi-
> cal parties do not exist, and where economic chaos caused by guerrilla action is
> edited out.[26]

Videos of guerrilla "victories" were shown to peasants in village plazas, often with the aid of truck battery power. Training videos were also made for

---

* It is interesting that, during President Lyndon Johnson's administration, a pilot Educational Television project, heavily funded by USAID, was instituted in El Salvador. The project, which ran from 1968–1972, trained El Salvadoran students at the grade 7–9 (ages roughly
13–15) level, aimed toward giving them future industrial and technical employment opportunities. The 7th grade enrollments increased 300% under this project, and the quality of the education of the group was judged to be increased by 15–25% over their non-ETV trained counter-
parts. At the end of the pilot period, however, a test survey by USAID showed that 50% of the
project's graduates lacked employment. This prompted the rather prophetic warning in
USAID's final report that " 'El Salvador may be in for trouble in the future if job opportunities
cannot be found for 9th grade graduates and aspirations are transferred into increased frustration and social unrest.' "[23] The youngsters trained by TV-age methods are now the perfect age
to be guerrillas — somewhere between their mid-20s and early 30s.[24]

fighters, showing them how to erect camouflage, how to perpetrate ambushes and silent infiltration, how to resist interrogation, and how to operate unfamiliar captured weapons. To counter poor relationships with the Catholic church and religious peasants, the *Times* says, the guerrillas also made a video, "Sowing Hope,"* that depicts scenes of armed guerrillas crossing themselves in front of a cross and taking communion from a Catholic priest."[27] The *Times* reported that video footage was being sold to CBS and various European TV networks.** Much of the equipment — of home video type — was paid for by European sympathizers. (The guerrillas complain that such home type equipment breaks down under the heavy use they give it.)

To gain a wider audience and influence American public opinion, the group had a video, "Time of Daring," premiered by Joseph Papp's 1984 Festival Latino en Nueva York. The group also secured an American distributor, Icarus,

> an independent film distributor in New York . . . [which planned, in August 1984] to mail 12,000 publicity brochures for the films to churches and college campuses across the United States.[28]†

These guerrilla photographic activities began about 1980, and were "inspired largely by a similar film project the Sandinista guerrillas in Nicaragua started a few weeks before the war there ended. . . ."[32] Nicaraguans and Cubans are said to have given advice on setting up the Salvadoran activity.

Corroboration of this story was sought from a personal contact familiar with the El Salvadoran situation, who said

> there can be little question about the fact that the guerrillas have picked up on video technology. I can't say just how many video crews they have running around the countryside recording their activities, but three does not seem an unreasonable number . . .

---

* Probably "Seedtime of Hope." See news release descriptions in later footnote.

** NBC Nightly News showed scenes from some of these guerrilla "home movies" on July 8, 1985.

† Icarus Films, with offices at 200 Park Avenue South, New York City, and at 22 Passage des Petites Ecuries in Paris, distributed news releases on March 15 and July 14, 1984.[29] Three guerrilla productions were pushed in the March 15th release:[30] "Decision to Win," made in 1981; "Letter from Morazan," made in 1982; and "Seedtime of Hope," made in 1983. Available in either 16 millimeter or on video, and for both sale and rental, the videos sold for $690, $540, and $260, respectively. The July 11 release was devoted entirely to "A Time of Daring," which included a number of scenes of American participation. This video, the release says, "was awarded the Grand Coral First Prize for Documentary Films at the 1983 Festival of New Latin American Cinema, held last December in Havana."[31] While the 16 millimeter version could be rented, the video was for sale only, the price being $400.

> I am not aware that the guerrillas are showing video tapes in village plazas, and, indeed, am a little skeptical on this topic, since many of the places where they spend their time are without electricity (generally as a result of their own handiwork).

> I know that they make extensive use of their video materials outside of El Salvador. They not only use the tapes to present their view of events, but are obviously picking up a modest piece of change on sales . . .

> Their own statements have made it clear that they consider their video and audio tapes to be the basis of a future history of the revolution.[33]*

In January 1985, the Salvadoran army apparently decided, "if you can't lick 'em, join 'em." The Arce Batallion in San Miguel Province rounded up 52 peasants charged with feeding Salvadoran rebels, hauled them in trucks to the military barracks, interrogated them, gave them political indoctrination, fed them, gave them medicine, and then treated them to a "string of movies on the Betamax video cassette produced by the psychological operations unit of the Salvadoran Army."[38] The movies were introduced by a

> hammer and sickle superimposed over Cuba [which] grew larger and larger until it filled the television screen. A deep male voice explained over ominous music on the soundtrack, how international communism was trying to take over El Salvador.[39]

Hopefully converted peasants were then returned by the Red Cross to the Sesori area, which had been "selected for the operation because Army intelligence had detected peasant unhappiness with the guerrillas' demands for food. . . ."[40] This *Christian Science Monitor* article said that "The Army hopes to exploit this resentment by creating a new image of the Army as the friend and protector of the peasants. . . ."[41]

On January 27, 1985, NBC Nightly News had an item saying that the El Salvadoran Army had again arrested a group of peasants, and again showed

---

*Conventional electricity is not mandatory to run a VCR. Many mentions of uses of alternate power sources — car and truck batteries, portable generators — were seen during this study. In Nigeria, the most popular videos "were those rugged long-playing machines that can be used with a portable electric power generator kit."[34] In Inner Mongolia, a sheep herdsman, benefitting from China's agricultural responsibility system, runs his new TV set on windmill power.[35] Professor Nora Quebral of the Philippines mentions the probability of rural entrepreneurs in her country showing cassettes to their neighbors for a few centavos, using VCRs "run on car batteries in places not blessed with electricity. . . ."[36] Anti-vivisectionist videocassettes shown using a generator have been seen in Harvard Square, Cambridge.[37] *The New York Times* article cited mentioned that the Salvadorans were using truck batteries for power in at least one instance.

them videos, this time of the Pope, stressing that the guerrillas were anti-Catholic.[42]*

USE OF VIDEOCASSETTES BY THE SUPERPOWERS IN AFGHANISTAN

A similar scenario to that in El Salvador is being followed by the superpowers in Afghanistan. *The Afghan Information Centre Bulletin* reported in October 1984 on how the Russians prepared a videotape in Kandahar for USSR home consumption:

> On September 22 a Russian army unit surrounded the building of the government agricultural department. Old army uniforms, mattresses and blankets were thrown inside the rooms, petrol was poured on the heaps and they were set on fire. At that moment a Russian TV team went into action. It filmed the building on fire and the Red Army fire brigade extinguishing it. Thus the Russians will see on their TV screens how the Afghan "bandits" are burning houses and how "the Soviets friendly armed forces" are "helping" the Afghan people.[44]

Another incident in Kandahar Province is said to have happened in June 1985. Russian commandoes are said to have invaded a village, causing about 20 women "running in panic from Russians who chased after them" to jump into a river and drown. During this raid, it is said, about 25 village elders were executed. Despite the carnage, a resistance fighter reported:

> " . . . the astonishing thing was that the Russians had brought with them cameramen who were filming and taking pictures of the horror scenes. Soviet soldiers forcefully dragged crying and shouting women in front of the cameras."[45]

The mystery of why they would do this was clarified when,

> on June 3 . . . the radio of Soviet Tajikistan . . . announced that when a unit of their glorious army clean the district of Qarghayee in Laghman from bandits and murderers, their reporters were witness to touching scenes: local women, weeping for joy, threw themselves in the arms of the friendly Soviet soldiers.[46]

In September 1985, the other superpower appeared ready to get into the act. *Time* magazine reported that the United States Information Agency

---

* U.S. mercenaries fighting in Nicaragua, who call themselves "Soldiers of Fortune," are also making video tapes of their exploits.[43]

(USIA) was "considering equipping Afghan 'freedom fighters' with mini-cams to film action footage of Soviet aggression."[47]

USE OF VIDEO IN PERU'S SHINING PATH SITUATION

In Peru, the military and police are said to have been killing Indian peasants thought to be linked to the Maoist Shining Path guerrilla movement.* The Shining Path began to escalate activities in 1982, and by 1983 had overwhelmed local police forces in some of Peru's southwestern provinces. *The New York Times* said that there is much talk of fighting terror with terror:

> Showing a videotape of mangled peasant bodies, a police chief at the Andean town of Ayacucho said: "The terrorists have the support of 80 percent of the Ayacucho people. What we need here is the Argentine solution." His view, reportedly shared by a number of senior military officers, was an allusion to the military campaign in Argentina in which thousands of armed guerrillas, unarmed sympathizers and peaceful opponents of the Government were killed.[50]

The purpose of this video was not mentioned, but it was said that disinformation was part of the military's strategy.

OFF-THE-AIR "HOW TO" FOR WOULD-BE ASSASSINS

John Hinkley was inspired to shoot President Reagan by the fictional movie, "Taxi Driver." A group of junior Pakistani Army officers apparently sought such inspiration from reality. In an aborted coup, scheduled for March 23, 1984, but uncovered that January,

> a videotape of an American television network's live coverage of the 1980 assassination of Egyptian leader Anwar Sadat was reportedly found at the Lahore home of an Army major, said to be a key member of the junior officers' group.[51]

---

* Members of Peru's *Sendero Luminoso*, or Shining Path: "are best described as orphans of the Gang of Four — Peruvian academicians and other highly trained intellectuals who had lived in China during the last years of Mao and who suddenly found themselves out in the cold. Back in Peru they worked at the University of Guamanga in Ayacucho, about 200 miles from Lima, and they established contact with the rural areas. What they had in mind was a Maoist insurrection with Indian roots — trying to blend both worlds."[48] Peasants who grow coca leaf for the black market, backed by the guerrillas, are the focus of a U.S.-backed anti-cocaine campaign. Coca brings the peasants five times the price of coffee, and the drug dealers get much, much more.[49] The drugs bring to Peru the income that permits the purchase of consumer products.

The coup attempt put heavy strains on Indian–Pakistani relations, since it involved the Indian Embassy's number three man, Counselor Arun Prashad. A former Indian police officer, Prashad was head of the research and analysis wing of Indian intelligence in Islamabad. He had gone to New Delhi for consultations, after which his household staff gained two Indian "servants." Under surveillance, these new domestics were found to be charged with seeing the necessary arms shipment for a coup safely across the Indian border. According to *The Christian Science Monitor*:

> on the night of Jan. 2 . . . a false-bottomed truck, containing a vast cache of arms, crossed the Pakistani border from India. The truck was followed by Pakistani security officials to the Army cantonment in Lahore.
>
> . . . the arms uncovered in the truck — and in a subsequent raid on the home of the major . . . possessing the videotape of the Sadat assassination, were sufficient to arm 200 to 300 men, and included ground-to-air missiles, antitank missiles, automatic repeater rifles, mortars, and plastique.[52]

The involved officers whose conspiracy "called for the assassination of General Zia . . . as he reviewed the March 23rd Republic Day parade,"[53] were said to be a "heterogeneous grouping of nationalists, socialists, and several devotees of Libyan President Muammar Qaddafi. . . ."[54] Egypt's Sadat was assassinated by fundamentalist Muslim troops who were part of the parade he was reviewing on October 6, 1981.

THE USE OF VIDEOCASSETTES BY MIDDLE EASTERN TERRORISTS

Tremendous television coverage was given to the activities of Shiite terrorists who hijacked TWA Flight 847 in summer 1985. In addition to press conferences which the terrorists held for the media with "their" American hostages, the terrorists also made and released to the news media their own videocassette productions. On June 25th, *The Boston Globe*, for instance, reported:

> Eight grim-looking hostages from TWA Flight 847, seen on a videotape received by US television networks yesterday, said they were well and hoped to be released soon.
>
> On the poor-quality videotape, the hostages apparently were answering questions from one of their captors, who asked each if he was being treated well. Each assented without visible enthusiasm, and few smiles were seen.[55]

When CBS obtained this at first exclusive footage from the Amal militia, it was accused by the other networks of paying the hijackers for it. David Fitzpatrick, who ran the CBS operation in Beirut, denied this, saying,

> the only thing Amal asked for in return was network footage of Israel's invasion of Lebanon, which he said CBS was willing to provide. Amal has been showing the hostages scenes of the destruction in an effort to win sympathy for the Lebanese cause.[56]

The furnishing of footage was quickly denied by a CBS News spokeswoman, who said, " 'We would never give footage to the Shiites or others requesting it.' "[57] The terrorists used videotapes, along with "lectures and late-night debates," to try to indoctrinate the hostages.[58]

Within a few days after the release of the American hostages in Beirut, two car bomb attacks in Southern Lebanon killed 17 people. A Syrian-backed group claimed credit. Before embarking upon their missions, the alleged suicide drivers, a Druse woman, Ibtissam Harb, and a Syrian-born man, Khaled Azrak, made videocassettes, testifying to their devotion to the terrorist cause and saying why the were dying for it. The videocassettes were made available by the National Syrian Socialist Party, a part of the Lebanese National Resistance Front.[59] Less than a week later, a third car, carrying a Red Cross flag, blew up at an Israeli checkpoint in Southern Lebanon, killing 10 people. The Lebanese radio proclaimed the terrorist operation " 'another heroic operation by Lebanese resistance fighters' "[60] and

> Lebanese television broadcast a prerecorded videotaped message from a man who identified himself as the suicide bomber and said he was acting on behalf of a pro-Syrian group called the Baath Party Organization of Lebanon.[61]

This group, also a part of the Lebanese National Resistance Front, is said to have links to the Syrian ruling Baath Party. *The New York Times* says:

> the purported suicide bomber in the incident today, who identified himself on the videotape as Hisham Abbas, a 22-year-old Lebanese, said his intention was to kill as many Israeli soldiers as possible. The man, who sat under a portrait of President Assad, said other suicide bombers were waiting their turn.[62]

The videocassettes were apparently an attempt to personalize the bombers and make the bombings appear like the rational acts of clean-cut people. One must take on faith, of course, that the persons shown in the videocassettes were the actual suicide drivers.

VIDEOS AND THE IRAN HOSTAGE CRISIS

At the end of 1980, during which Walter Cronkite had nightly counted off how long Americans had been held as Iranian hostages, and during which Iran's revolutionary government had received massive worldwide publicity,* Scott Kraft of AP expressed American sentiments, saying in a yearly overview,

> we hoped through all 31,622,400 seconds that a bearded religious man would set free 52 of us [Americans] held hostage in a distant land. We enter the next year still hoping.[64]

The hostages were finally freed on Inauguration Day, 1981 — but not before "farewell" videos had been taken. These tapes, the last of several made of the hostages and fed from time to time by satellite via U.S. networks to the American people, consisted of interviews in which each hostage was required to say, before release, that he or she had not been mistreated.[65]

The authors have previously described how the three American networks obtained the "students' " Easter 1980 video of the hostages, and relayed it to the U.S. The first chain in the linkup of the involved satellite systems was the microwave the Iranian government had provided between the American Embassy and Iran's television, Voice and Vision of the Islamic Republic (VVIR).[66] Painful as that Easter videotape was — and was meant to be by the Iranian captors — the videographers outdid themselves with their Christmas special eight months later. *United Press International* reported:

> the Iranian videotape was made Christmas Eve during an all-night visit by the Vatican's representative to Iran and several Iranian clergymen. . . .[67]

During the 40-minute tape, which showed 27 of the 52 hostages, the following were among the scenes shown:

> Hostage Kathryn L. Koob asked her relatives back in the United States to sing along with her . . . and softly began, her voice breaking, "Be near me Lord Jesus, I ask you to stay. . . ."

---

* Robert Friedlander, Professor of Law at Ohio Northern University, has pointed out that, while each of the U.S. television networks produced less than a story a week on the 1978 Iranian Revolution, during 1979 and especially after the Embassy was seized, CBS showed 252 stories, ABC 261 stories, and NBC 208 stories devoted to Iran. *The Washington Post,* he says, had carried 35 articles on Iran in 1977 and 134 articles in 1978, but increased this to 476 articles after the hostages were taken. During 1980, the *Post* "carried a total of 916 articles, or an average of nearly 3 a day . . . " *The New York Times Index,* cursorily examined, he says, indicated an even larger coverage.[63] At least some portion of this was a result of the "student" captors' skillful video usage.

[Barry Rosen of New York City said,] "To my dear mother, I want you to know my thoughts were with you during Rosh Hashanah and Chanukah and the . . . happy memories we used to share with the family together . . . "

Robert Belk . . . of West Columbia, S.C. said that although his family "is not receiving much of my mail, and I'm certainly not receiving much of their mail, I am all right and do expect to come home — when I don't know."[68]

The fun and games might have gone on forever, but with the Shah dead (his admission to an American hospital having precipitated the Embassy takeover), a debilitating war with Iraq raging, and the care of the hostages presenting a growing burden, they were finally released a few weeks later.

OLD VITRIOL IN NEW BOTTLES

In the early 1980s, Eugene Terre Blanche, a 37-year-old farmer and former policeman, began spreading his antisemitic message by videocassette throughout the Transvaal. Terre Blanche headed the Afrikaner Resistance Movement, which "holds that all political parties must be abolished if South Africa is to be saved as a white, Christian nation from the forces of the Antichrist."[69] *The New York Times* reports:

> Mr. Terre Blanche says that the Antichrist in South Africa is represented by the "money powers," notably mining conglomerates such as the giant Anglo-American Corporation and its chairman, Harry F. Oppenheimer. [Terre Blanche says that] The governing National Party has deserted the Afrikaner cause . . . and is now totally in the grips of this infernal force.[70]

The article also says that,

> in separate interviews . . . [Terre Blanche] and the movement's national secretary, Jan Groenewald, a former security policeman, said that they saw the "money powers" as a front for "international Zionism", which in turn, they said, is dedicated to destroying white South Africa.

The group's flag and the little pins it gives out to audiences sport lopsided swastika-like figures.

A "theatrical presence on the podium," Terre Blanche had, by 1981, sold 30,000 copies of his speeches on audiocassettes. He took to videocassettes, so as to reach many more people through showings at small private house meetings than he ever could meet with personally.*

---

* In July 1983, Terre Blanche, Groenewald, David Botes, organizing secretary for their group and a "Springs town councillor," as well as a founding member of the group, Jacob Daniel

David Calvert Smith of the U.S. is said to be distributing copies of anti-Jewish hate films made in the heyday of Nazi Propaganda Minister Joseph Goebbels to ultra-right-wing groups in this country.[72] He is also said to be guilty of piracy. His activities came to light when Transit Films of Munich, distributor of 1926–1945 films for the Friedrich Wilhelm Murnau Stiftung (Foundation), sought to keep Smith from violating the Foundation's copyright. Smith distributes through companies with names like Kulturfilmwerks Corp., Condor Films Inc., German Film Bureau International, Educational Services Administration, etc., which "crop up in such places as Los Angeles or Dallas and are constantly changing addresses or names. . . ."[73] *Variety* says that "Smith and . . . others evidently obtained the prints . . . from private collectors, some of whom may have brought them back as war booty from World War II."[74]

VIDEOCASSETTES AS ELECTRONIC NEWS RELEASES AND OTHER TOOLS TO ASSIST IN LOBBYING

The newest political game in town is to have videotapes prepared which will get you TV coverage. These "electronic news releases" are delivered by mail or by satellite to local television stations and the Cable News Network.[75] A growing number of public relations firms are being paid to prepare what look like legitimate news items, but are really lobbying efforts for some specific paying client. Gray & Company, of Washington, D.C.,* came under fire from the Justice Department in spring 1985 when it prepared and distributed such materials for foreign clients without registering as a foreign agent. Prior to the meeting of President Reagan and Japanese Prime Minister Nakasone in early 1985, Gray distributed "news" reports showing U.S. produce being shipped to Japan, and featuring the U.S. Ambassador to Japan, Mike Mansfield, saying that " 'Japanese markets aren't as closed as we might think.' "[77] This "news item" was, however, paid for by the government of Japan, and was directed ultimately — via local U.S. television viewers — at the U.S. Congress. *The Wall Street Journal* says

---

Viljoen, were arrested: "in connection with the discovery of a cache of arms, including several AK 47 rifles, thousands of rounds of ammunition, a 20-mm rocket, anti-personnel mines and several camouflage outfits . . . which were found on the farm of Terre Blanche's brother."[71] Viljoen had already been sentenced to 15 years in June for assisting group plans to "assassinate black churchmen and commit acts of sabotage against multi-racial hotels." Terre Blanche had also received an 18-month suspended sentence for a different charge of illegal arms possession. Among other accusations against the African Resistance Movement members was that they planned to attack Bishop Desmond Tutu.

  * Gray & Company is owned by Robert K. Gray, the co-chairman of the Reagan Inaugural Committee.[76]

Japan was interested in de-emphasizing America's $35 billion trade deficit with that country and preventing the passage of U.S. legislation aimed to restrict Japanese imports.[78]

Another Gray production featured a former Washington, D.C. WTTG-TV anchorwoman (later a Gray vice president) holding an exclusive interview in Morocco with that country's King Hassan II. In this instance,

as . . . [the "reporter"] listened, the King advised the United States not to worry about his country's recent treaty with Libyan leader Moammar Khadafy. The sentiment was reinforced in a standup conclusion . . . [the "reporter"] did outside the palace: "The political fallout from the Treaty may not yet be over, but any harsh reaction from the West must be tempered with the acknowledgment that Morocco is strategically important to the United States, and that in this part of the world, strong pro-American leaders are hard to find". . . .[79]

Gray & Company has a minimum budget of $360,000 supplied by the Moroccan government to say such nice things about Morocco.[80]

The Wall Street Journal said that these videotape packages may be sent to local TV stations by mail, or by way of communications satellites, and a package

typically includes pieces that can be run immediately as well as interviews and background shots that can be combined with a news staff's own reporting.[81]

Devices used to make the pieces look like "news" rather than public relations are:

- Hiring TV personages with name recognition to do them.
- Having professional journalists using pseudonyms do them.
- Blurring the "reporter's" identity and whereabouts, or keeping the "reporter's" lines as a voice-over off camera.
- Leaving labels off the tapes, so each station can insert its own typeface to make it look like its own reporting.
- Having a dark blonde "reporter" do the interview with back to camera. (" 'Every station has a reporter with dark blonde hair,' " says one article.)[82]

These foreign lobbying efforts, as well as all sorts of domestic commercial propaganda, may not even be labeled as such. But even if they are, small stations on small budgets (and sometimes larger ones) often use the material. A Detroit news director is quoted as saying " 'We're a small operation and can't cover things outside of the metropolitan area. Anyway, all stories are slanted to some extent.' "[83]

The flooding of local TV stations with videocassettes — made easy by cheap satellite communications — is also taken advantage of by the U.S. Congress. In 1983, the Bonneville Satellite Corporation installed transmission facilities "on the edge of Capital Hill" to transmit messages. The *Washington Journalism Review* says:

> every day Congress is in session, growing numbers of senators and representatives routinely offer news clips of their activities via satellite to stations in their home states, with the taxpayer picking up most of the tab. Advances in satellite communications in the past few years have made it simple and economical for the average member of Congress to bypass Washington reporters and beam his message to a local and often more accommodating press corps. The footage often appears on local TV newscasts with no explanation to viewers that it was shot for and supplied by the senator or congressman it features.[84]

The House still uses fixed cameras, but the Senate keeps "at least three" minicam crews busy.[85]

There are those who say that the electronic press release is no different from the ordinary print release, but the detractors of electronic news releases say the power of the picture and the deliberate tailoring to look like "real news" render these videocassettes the bearers of more powerful political messages.[86]

Gray & Company also uses videocassettes to help foreign lobbyists prepare for congressional hearings and other appearances. For instance, that company got $10,000 to help the deputy chairman of the Kuwait Petroleum Company with his presentation to Representative Rosenthal's Government Operations Subcommittee. This included a critique of a videotape of Abdul Razzak Mohammed Mulla Hussain "presenting his statement and anticipated potential questions from members of the House panel. . . ."[87] *U.S. News and World Report* says that lobbying by foreigners in the United States by various means is now a more than $100 million business.[88]

THE USE OF VIDEOCASSETTES TO FRUSTRATE GOVERNMENT EFFORTS AT TV CENSORSHIP

In August 1985, the British Broadcasting Corporation (BBC) canceled the broadcast of a documentary concerning the Irish Republican Army (IRA), "At the Edge of the Union," bowing

> to public pressure from Prime Minister Margaret Thatcher and Home Secretary Leon Brittan to keep the show off the air because it might provide 'succor to terrorism". . . .[89]

and making infamous Thatcher's earlier statement that

> Democratic nations "must try to find ways to starve the terrorist and the hijacker of the oxygen of publicity on which they depend". . . .[90]

BBC journalists went on strike for a day in protest, silencing its "highly respected World Service for [the] first time in its 53 year history."[91] Videotapes of the canceled documentary were immediately thrown into the breach, with

> leaked copies of the film being shown by journalist pickets on a television set in the streets of Belfast, and in small viewing theaters in Birmingham and London.[92]

The strike ended when agreement was reached to show a slightly altered version of the documentary the following October.[93] But, as a result of this incident and other pressures on BBC by the government, Assistant Director General Alan Protheroe, in an October speech, called for a British Bill of Rights and a Freedom of Information Act patterned on those in use in the United States.[94]

VIDEO IN LIEU OF VISA

Three interesting cases of the use of videocassettes when visas had been denied were discovered during the study. The first involved South African Bishop Desmond Tutu, who was denied exit from that country; the second involved United States AFL-CIO President, Lane Kirland, who was denied entry into Poland; and the third involved two Cuban officials who were not permitted to enter the United States.

In August 1981, Anglican Bishop Desmond Tutu was scheduled to address the biennial meeting of the Disciples of Christ in Anaheim, California. But before leaving South Africa, he made a straw-that-broke-the-camel's-back statement that caused the South African government to lift his passport and to investigate the 13-million strong South African Council of Churches, headed since 1978 by Tutu. Unable to come himself to Anaheim, Bishop Tutu instead sent a videotape to supplement the empty chair reserved for him. In the video, he twice said the same thing "that got him into trouble," that is, that "the South African government's attempt to put blacks into segregated 'homelands' is the worst travesty since Naziism."[95] Tutu has for many year been a leader in the battle against apartheid, which since 1948 has been South African policy.[96] After charging Tutu and his Council with "waging 'massive psychological warfare' against the government and sympathizing with outlawed liberation groups such as the Zambia-based African National Congress,"[97] the South African government has ever since kept his passport, but it has been unable to silence the voluble bishop. Tutu, who won the Nobel Prize in fall 1984, now travels frequently, but under special arrangements.

About a month after Bishop Tutu was denied exit to the United States, and three months before Solidarity was crushed, U.S. president of the AFL-CIO, Lane Kirkland and other U.S. labor officials were denied visas to enter Poland. Kirkland had been invited to address the meeting of the Solidarity Congress at Gdansk. Incensed "that the Polish government would deny Solidarity its right, as a free and independent union, to decide who will attend its convention,"[98] Kirkland, pledging continuing support for the Polish union, sent along a videotape of his planned speech " 'in the hope that it will reach Solidarity.' "[99] In the video, Kirkland said the Solidarity movement had

"not only brought 'renewal' to Poland. You have renewed the spirit of workers throughout the world."

"You have transformed the word 'Solidarity' from a slogan to a living moral force that has galvanized the universal cause of free and independent trade unionism". . .

"For all who believe in peaceful relations among states, there is no task more urgent than unlinking human rights and freedom from the question of who owns the means of production" . . .[100]

The AFL-CIO had been sending "printing equipment and other supplies" to Solidarity, and had raised "about $250,000" for its aid.[101]

No information is available on whether the videocassette reached its destination.

Also in September 1981, two Cuban officials, Alberto Betancourt Roa of the Ministry of Foreign Trade, and Marcelo Fernandez Font, advisor to the Cuban Central Planning Board, were denied visas by the U.S. State Department. *The Associated Press* reported that

The officials circumvented the visa denials by providing videotaped remarks to [a] seminar, sponsored by two local universities and the Center for Cuban Studies in New York, a private research group. Most of the participants in the two-day seminar, which included several congressmen, favor a more conciliatory U.S. policy toward Cuba. The seminar, held in a House office building, also featured brief remarks by the head of the Cuban diplomatic mission here, Ramon Sanchez Parodi. The analysis of the Cuban economy by the two officials contrasted sharply with that of the State Department, which claims Cuba is afflicted by chronic shortages and is almost totally dependent on the Soviet Union for its survival.[102]

The officials, in their video, painted a picture of a thriving Cuban economy, in which foreign trade had increased six-fold since the revolution, more than 100 new trade items had been developed, and a growth rate of 4% a year had been maintained with 5% expected, and they predicted a per capita income increase of 15 to 20% for the period 1981–1985.

According to *The Associated Press*:

> their [the officials'] presentations minimized the role of the Soviet Union in the Cuban economy. American officials estimate the annual Soviet subsidy at about $2 billion a year or roughly $300 for every Cuban man, woman and child.[103]

The United States has had a trade embargo against Cuba since the Kennedy administration.

FURTHER USES OF VIDEOTAPES BY GOVERNMENTS

The U.S. and the KAL 007 incident. *   When Korean Airlines Flight 007 was downed by the Russians on September 1, 1983, the television division of the United States Information Agency (USIA) hastened to put together a videocassette that discussed the incident and included recordings of the voices of the Soviet pilots. This was played to a packed Security Council Chamber at the United Nations during the heated debates following the downing. The purpose of the video was to " 'put the lie to the Soviet case'. . . ."[105] To make the point more explicitly, "One of the television sets was installed directly behind the Soviet delegation."[106] After the showing,

---

* This video is remarkable for being created for the occasion. All United States Information Service (USIS) posts around the world have VCR equipment and individual libraries of cassettes suitable to support a range of issue areas from American culture and society to American policy in economic, political, and military affairs. These tapes are available for screening in USIS libraries and centers, for invitational screenings at Embassies and officers' homes, and sometimes for loan to key members of the host society. For years, CBS nightly news has been pouched to American embassies in various posts, and screening of this news, even when several days old, is said to be a major socializing event between the local press corps and USIS officers. Worldnet, the recently established USIA television feed to a large number of American posts, now sends ABC-TV news to them by satellite, for videotaping on arrival. A 72-hour wait before use is still required, for business, not technical reasons, but the news is much fresher than the pouched variety. It is therefore more capable, it is said, of acting as a counter to the "news service" provided by the USSR's TASS, which is relied on by the press corps in such countries as Tanzania. Since the early 1980s, USIA has also been using "video teleconferencing." Teleconferences between USIS posts and policymakers or cultural celebrities are supplemented by a previously taped and pouched interview or statement of the scheduled caller, to give the phone voice—cheaply—a human dimension. The tape can also be shown prior to teleconference so participants can prepare country-specific "follow-up" questions.[104]

U.S. Ambassador Jeane Kirkpatrick told reporters that "the airing of the tape prompted the Kremlin to admit shooting down the plane."[107] In the days following the downing, the story of "the Soviet shooting down of the Korean jet with 269 aboard 'has been the lead story in all 42 languages on Voice of America'. . . ."[108]

Later, the USIA "prepared a 30-minute tape that contain[ed] television news reports from seven countries — Canada, New Zealand, Chile, Australia, Sweden, and Japan"[109] — to be aired at 51 U.S. embassies. Embassies had also been provided, at the height of the crisis, with videotapes of the "McNeill-Lehrer Report," "ABC's Nightline," and a number of other shows, which were to be used "to keep American workers informed, to be shown to foreign government leaders and . . . [maybe] offered to local broadcasters . . ."[110]

The Indian crisis in the Punjab.   During the summer of 1984, the Indian government produced some videocassettes to support its stand on the Punjab issue and to defend the Indian Army's attack on the Sikhs' Golden Temple. These cassettes were given to many Congress-I leaders and to diplomats leaving for overseas assignments. The Indian embassies abroad were asked to show the videocassettes to selected audiences of Indians overseas, especially those of the Sikh religion.[111]

The Sakharov tapes.   In August 1984, *Bild Zeitung,* a West German daily newspaper, obtained a 20-minute videotape of Soviet human rights activist Andrei Sakharov and his wife Yelena Bonner.[112] Nobel Prize-winning Sakharov, who had been banished without trial to Gorky, off-limits to foreigners, had been on a prolonged hunger strike to protest the Soviets' refusal to allow his wife to seek medical attention outside the country.* At the time of the release of the video, it had been reported that Yelena Bonner had just been convicted of "slandering the Soviet state"[113] and had been sentenced to five years of internal exile.

There was speculation at the U.S. State Department that the videotape was intended to divert attention from the trial, as well as to show that Sakharov was both alive and well, both of which, in recent months, had been doubted.[114] The source of the videocassette was identified as Victor Louis, who in June had supplied some still photographs of Sakharov. Louis, says *The New York Times,* is "a London-based Soviet journalist whom Moscow often uses to leak information to the west."[115] A personal contact for the Soviet Union has commented that the videocassette was clearly an official KGB product. The Russians wanted publicity for their viewpoint, the contact said, and, when still pictures didn't work, they tried video.[116]

Following discussions in the world press that the Sakharovs were not

---

* During the thaw in US/Soviet relations at the time of the fall 1985 Summit, Bonner was permitted to come to Italy and the U.S. for medical treatment.

shown together in the videocassette, Louis delivered to *Bild Zeitung* eight more still pictures.[117] Seven of these, which the Russians obviously hoped would stop that set of rumors, showed both of the Sakharovs. Other Sakharov tapes of a similar nature were released by the same sources on later occasions.

The use of hypothetical videotapes.   A number of cases have turned up in which authorities *say* they have a videotape incriminating a person or group, but the tape is never, in fact, brought forward.

Following the introduction of martial law in Poland at the end of 1981, broadcasts on the program "Moscow in English for North America" took the U.S. to task for saying that the Soviets were involved in this. A broadcast picked up by BBC said:

> Washington certainly knows what is now common knowledge, and that is that martial law was introduced because a state coup had been in the offing . . . The documents confiscated from Solidarity prove this . . . These documents, and also statements made by the interned Solidarity leaders, called for mass terror and violence . . . The armed overthrow against the state was scheduled for 17th December. Caches of arms, fuel and food have been discovered . . . Anti-socialist literature has been found in abundance, and also tapes and video tapes with recorded messages by Solidarity leaders to be broadcast immediately after the overthrow of the government in office.[118]

Moscow did not say how it came to know so much about Polish business. The implementation of martial law in Poland came about in part because of resolutions passed at the fall Solidarity Congress. Theses 31 and 32 of these resolutions dealt specifically with demands for free access to information, and Item 7 of Thesis 32 said:

> The union will set up its own information, photographic, videotape, film and phonographic agencies and press publications. The union authorities should take action to set up its central press and information agency on general principles.[19]

During June 1980 riots in South Africa, foreign reporters were banned from entering the black townships. Colonel Leon Mellet, the head of the South African Police Directorate of Public Relations, said that this was because some of the foreign TV reporters had incited the black residents to riot. He claimed to have a video showing an unidentified cameraman giving "a black power salute,"[120] but declined to produce his evidence.

In August 1982, then Philippine President Ferdinand Marcos claimed to have thwarted a "plot to organize strikes, bombings and assassinations aimed at bringing down his government."[121] In a televised interview,

Marcos said that "businessmen, clergymen and journalists were linked to the conspiracy and members of the established opposition were involved in sub-version."[122] He said that " 'The evidence is there' " and that it included "video-tapes of conversations by some opposition members with terrorist and subversives."[123] He declined, however, to show the tapes, saying, "I wish I could tell the secrets. . . ."[124]

NOTES

[1]Nora C. Quebral, *The Video Recorder in Developing Countries,* speech, International Institute of Communications 1984 Annual Conference, Berlin, September 22, 1984, p. 4.

[2]Robert Trumbull, "Videotapes of Slaying Smuggled Into Manila," *The New York Times,* September 13, 1983, p. A-9.

[3]*Ibid.*

[4]The Philippines. Personal communications.

[5]"U.S. Filipinos Sending Home Published Attacks on Marcos," *The New York Times,* February 7, 1984, p. A-10.

[6]*Ibid.*

[7]Vincente T. Paterno, "Aquino's Death Gave Life to His Country," *The Wall Street Journal,* August 27, 1984, p. 13.

[8]*Ibid.*, and also:

Paul Gigot, "Filipino Voters Break Out of the Third-World Mold," *The Wall Street Journal,* May 21, 1984, p. 31.

[9]Many sources, including:

Harry Anderson, Melinda Liu, and Richard Vokey, "Did the Military Kill Aquino?" *Newsweek,* September 3, 1984, pp. 42–43.

"Probe Into Aquino Slaying Ends After Year-long Investigation," *The Washington Post,* October 24, 1984, p. A-22.

"Excerpts Form Majority's Report on Assassination of Aquino," *The New York Times,* October 25, 1984, p. A-16.

Pico Iyer and Sandra Burton, "The Heart of the Matter. A Report Accuses the Military in Aquino's Murder," *Time,* October 22, 1984, pp. 61–62.

[10]Fernando Del Mundo, "Airport Cameras Missed Aquino Killing," *United Press International,* November 15, 1983 (NEXIS).

Fernando Del Mundo, "No Video of Aquino Killing," *United Press International,* November 17, 1983 (NEXIS).

[11]*Ibid.*

[12]Fernando Del Mundo, "Airport Cameras Missed Aquino Killing," *United Press International,* November 15, 1983 (NEXIS).

[13]Fernando Del Mundo "Dateline: Manila," *United Press International,* August 14, 1984 (NEXIS).

[14]*Ibid.*

[15]Harry Anderson, Melinda Liu, and Richard Vokey, "Did the Military Kill Aquino?", *Newsweek,* September 3, 1984, pp. 42–43.

[16]Pico Iyer and Sandra Burton, "The Heart of the Matter. A Report Accuses the Military in Aquino's Murder," *Time,* October 22, 1984, pp. 61–62.

[17]Guy Sacerdoti, "Tearing up Agrava. Ver and Other Accused Are Found Innocent," *Far Eastern Economic Review,"* December 12, 1985, p. 14.

[18]*Excerpts from Majority's Report on Assassination of Aquino,"* *The New York Times,* October 25, 1984, p. A-16.

[19]Guy Sacerdoti, "Tearing Up Agrava. Ver and Other Accused Are Found Innocent," *Far Eastern Economic Review,"* December 12, 1985, p. 13.

[20]*Ibid.*

[21]*Ibid.*

[22]*Ibid.*

[23]Robert Hornick et al., *Television and Educational Reform in El Salvador,* final report, RT No. 14, USAID, August, 1973, p. 135. (In John H. Clippinger, *Who Gains by Communications Development? Studies In Information Technologies in Developing Countries,* Program on Information Resources Policy, Harvard University, January 1976, p. 44).

[24]John H. Clippinger, *Who Gains By Communications Development? Studies In Information Technologies in Developing Countries,* Program on Information Resources Policy, Harvard University, January 1976, pp. 41-42.

[25]James Brooke, "Salvadorans Use Video in the Propaganda War," *The New York Times,* August 27, 1984, p. C-17.

[26]*Ibid.*

[27]*Ibid.*

[28]*Ibid.*

[29]*A Time of Daring,* and *Reports from Inside El Salvador. 3 Films Produced by Radio Venceremos/ FLMN.* News Releases, Icarus Films, New York and Paris, July 11, 1984 and March 15, 1984.

[30]*Reports From Inside El Salvador. 3 films produced by Radio Venceremos/FMLN.* News Release, Icarus Films, New York and Paris, March 15, 1984.

[31]*A Time of Daring.* News Release, Icarus Films, New York and Paris, July 11, 1984.

[32]James Brooke, "Salvadorans Use Video in the Propaganda War," *The New York Times,* August 27, 1984, p. C-17.

[33]El Salvador. Personal communications.

[34]Segun Olusola, "The Video Shock," *InterMedia,* July/Sept. 1983, p. 64.

[35]Christopher S. Wren, "TV (and With it the World) Comes to Mongolians," *The New York Times,* November 14, 1984, p. 2.

[36]Nora C. Quebral, *The Video Recorder in Developing Countries,* Speech, International Institute of Communications 1984 Annual Conference, Berlin, September 22, 1984, p. 2.

[37]Personal observation of the authors.

[38]Chris Norton, "Salvador Army Shows Anticommunist Movies to Lure Peasants to Their Side," *The Christian Science Monitor,* January 24, 1985, p. 7.

[39]*Ibid.*

[40]*Ibid.*

[41]*Ibid.*

[42]NBC Nightly News, January 27, 1985.

[43]NBC Nightly News, October 1, 1984.

For Soldier of Fortune activities, see also:

"US Magazine Distributing CIA Manual on Nicaragua," *The Christian Science Monitor,* January 25, 1985, p. 2.

[44]"Kandahar. Growing Resistance in Unity and Strength (sic)," *Afghan Information Centre Monthly Bulletin,* October 1984, p. 9.

[45]"Resistance Offensive in Western Provinces. Kandahar," *Afghan Information Centre Monthly Bulletin,* June 1985, p. 7.

[46]*Ibid.*

[47]Evan Thomas, John Kohan and Alessandra Stanley, "The Great War of Words. How the U.S. and U.S.S.R. Sell Themselves to the World," *Time,* September 9, 1985, p. 33.

[48]Enrique Zileri, "Peru's Internal War. A Latin American Democracy's Struggle Against Terrorism," *World Press Review,* December 1984, pp. 28–30.

[49]Pamela Constable, "Peru Rebels, Drug Traders Hinder Anti-Cocaine Drive," *The Boston Globe,* February 17, 1985, p. 1.

Pamela Constable, "Uprooting Coca in Jungle is Hard, Dangerous Work," *The Boston Globe,* February 17, 1985, p. 20.

[50]Marlise Simons, "Peruvian Military Fights Terrorists with Terror," *The New York Times,* September 2, 1984, p. E-5.

[51]Mary Anne Weaver, "Failed Coup Against Pakistan Leader May Have Involved India," *The Christian Science Monitor,* March 19, 1984, p. 9.

[52]*Ibid.*

[53]*Ibid.*

[54]*Ibid.*

[55]"Eight Grim-Looking Hostages Give Short Answers in Taped Interviews," *The Boston Globe,* June 25, 1985, p. 3.

[56]Curtis Wilkie, "Covering Beirut Chaotic, Cutthroat," *The Boston Globe,* June 26, 1985, p. 14.

[57]*Ibid.*

[58]"Hijackers Called 'Thieves, Thugs and Murderers'," *The Boston Globe,* July 3, 1985, p. 2. Among other articles mentioning the use of videocassettes during the hijacking crisis were: Ed Siegel, "TV: A Prime Player in the Drama," *The Boston Globe,* June 26, 1985, p. 1.

Dan Goodgame, " 'An Attack on Civilization' Hostage Taking, Bombings and Killings Mark a Week of Phantasmagoric Terror," *Time,* July 1, 1985, p. 8.

[59]"15 Reported Killed in Israeli Raid on Palestinian Bases in Lebanon," *The Boston Globe,* July 11, 1985, p. 9.

[60]"3rd Car Explosion in South Lebanon in A Week Kills 10. Vehicle with Red Cross Flag Blows Up in Israeli Zone — Beirut Radio Hails Act," *The New York Times,* July 16, 1985, p. A-1.

[61]*Ibid.*

[62]*Ibid.*

[63]Robert A. Friedlander, "Iran: The Hostage Seizure, the Media, and the International Law," in *Terrorism. The Media and the Law.* Abraham H. Miller, ed., Transitional Publishers, Inc., Dobbs Ferry, NY, 1982, pp. 59–60.

[64]Scott Kraft, "1980: A Year of Hostages, Inflation, Nature's Fury," *The Associated Press,* December 17, 1980 (NEXIS).

[65]James Dalgleish, "Dateline: Tehran," "Iran," *Reuters,* January 28, 1981 (NEXIS).

[66]Oswald H. Ganley and Gladys D. Ganley, *To Inform or to Control? The New Communications Networks,* McGraw-Hill, New York, 1982, p. 67.

[67]Mel Laytner, "Hostages-Television" *United Press International,* December 26, 1980 (NEXIS).

[68]*Ibid.*

[69]Joseph Lelyveld, "Extremist South African Group Arouses Concern, *The New York Times,* August 23, 1981, p. A-3.

[70]*Ibid.*

[71]Richard Roy, "Two Whites Convicted of Terrorism," *United Press International,* June 13, 1983, (NEXIS).

See also:

"Right-Wing Leader to Face Terrorism Charges," *Reuters,* July 13, 1983 (NEXIS).

"Afrikaner Extremist," *Reuters,* June 24, 1983 (NEXIS).

"Foreign News Briefs, Klerksdorp, South Africa," *United Press International,* June 24, 1983 (NEXIS).

"Resistance," *Reuters,* December 14, 1982 (NEXIS).

"Right Wing Afrikaners Arrests," *United Press International,* December 11, 1982 (NEXIS).

[72]Jack Kindred, "Transit Film Seeks Halt to U.S. Piracy of Nazi Propaganda Pics," *Variety,* October 31, 1984, p. 32.

[73]*Ibid.*

[74]*Ibid.*

[75]Jeanne Saddler, "Public Relations Firms Offer 'News' to TV. Electronic Releases Contain Subtle Commercials for Clients," *The Wall Street Journal,* April 2, 1985, p. 6.

Paul Harris, "JD Calls Flack On the Carpet Over TV Feeds," *Variety,* April 3, 1985, p. 49.

[76]Kathryn Johnson, "Foreign Lobbyists—The Way They Operate in Washington," *U.S. News & World Report,* March 29, 1985, p. 41.

[77]Jeanne Saddler, "Public Relations Firms Offer 'News' to TV. Electronic Releases Contain Subtle Commercials for Clients," *The Wall Street Journal,* April 2, 1985, p. 6.

[78]*Ibid.*

[79]Mary Battiata, "Trouble Spots in Public Relations-Journalism Connections," *The Boston Globe,* March 31, 1985, p. A-96.

[80]*Ibid.*

[81]Jeanne Saddler, "Public Relations Firms Offer 'News' to TV. Electronic Releases Contain Subtle Commercials for Clients," *The Wall Street Journal,* April 2, 1985, p. 6.

[82]Paul West, "The Video Connection. Beaming It Straight to the Constituents," *Washington Journalism Review,* June 1985, pp. 48–50.

[83]Jeanne Saddler, "Public Relations Firms Offer 'News' to TV. Electronic Releases Contain Subtle Commercials for Clients," *The Wall Street Journal,* April 2, 1985, p. 6.

[84]Paul West, "The Video Connection. Beaming It Straight to the Constituents," *Washington Journalism Review,* June 1985, pp. 48–50.

[85]*Ibid.*

[86]*Ibid.*

[87]Kathryn Johnson, "Foreign Lobbyists—The Way They Operate in Washington," *U.S. News & World Report,* March 29, 1985, p. 41.

[88]*Ibid.*

[89]"BBC to Air Altered Version of Film on IRA; Strike Ends," *The Boston Globe,* August 8, 1985, p. 39.

[90]R. W. Apple, Jr., "Thatcher Urges the Press to Help 'Starve' Terrorists," *The New York Times,* July 16, 1985, p. A-3.

[91]"BBC Journalists End One-Day Strike," (photo caption), *The Boston Globe,* August 8, 1985, p. 3.

[92]"BBC. Confusion Confounded," *The Economist,* August 10, 1985, p. 40.

[93]"BBC to Air Altered Version of Film on IRA; Strike Ends," *The Boston Globe,* August 8, 1985, p. 39.

[94]Alan Protheroe, "The Broadcaster's Greatest Hazard is Fear," *Index on Censorship,* Volume 15, Number 1, January 1986, pp. 15–17.

[95]"Empty Chair for Tutu at Religious Gathering," *The Associated Press,* August 4, 1981 (NEXIS).

[96]William E. Smith, "Wrestling the Tiger," *Time,* September 24, 1984, pp. 34–36.

[97]Richard N. Ostling, "Searching for New Worlds, Honors Celebrate Eight Remarkable Achievers," *Time,* October 29, 1984, p. 62.

[98]"Kirkland–Solidarity. Dateline: Washington," *The Associated Press,* September 26, 1981 (NEXIS).

[99]*Ibid.*

[100]*Ibid.*

[101]*Ibid.*

102George Gedda, "Cuban Officials Paint Bright Economic Picture," *The Associated Press,* September 23, 1981 (NEXIS).

103*Ibid.*

104Richard Bissell and others. Personal communications.

105Randolph E. Schmid, "U.S. Steps Up Broadcasts to Soviets," *The Associated Press,* September 8, 1983 (NEXIS).

106*Ibid.*

107John Usher, "UN. Dateline: United Nations," *United Press International,* September 6, 1983 (NEXIS).

108Randolph E. Schmid, "U.S. Steps Up Broadcasts to Soviets, "*The Associated Press,* September 8, 1983 (NEXIS).

109"Dateline: Washington," *United Press International,* September 30, 1983 (NEXIS).

110Randolph E. Schmid, "U.S. Steps Up Broadcasts to Soviets," *The Associated Press,* September 8, 1983 (NEXIS).

111India. Personal communications.

112Many sources, including:

William Scally, "Sakharov–American. Dateline: Washington," *Reuters,* August 23, 1984 (NEXIS).

"Dateline: Washington," *Reuters,* August 23, 1984 (NEXIS) (second article).

CBS Evening News, August 23, 1984.

"A KGB Home Movie," *Newsweek,* September 3, 1984, p. 49.

113William Scally, "Sakharov–American. Dateline: Washington, *Reuters,* August 23, 1984 (NEXIS).

See also:

Bernard Gwertzman, "Moscow Said to Banish Bonner for State Slander," *The New York Times,* August 24, 1984, p. A-4.

114*Ibid.*

115"Paper Says Videotape Shows Sakharov Is Fit," *The New York Times,* August 23, 1984, p. A-8.

116The Soviet Union. Personal communications.

117NBC Nightly News, December 14, 1984.

118"US Allegations of Soviet Involvement in Poland 'Pure Provocation' ", text of commentary by Vladislav Kozyakov, Moscow in English for North America, 21 December 1981, *British Broadcasting Corporation; Summary of World Broadcasts,* December 23, 1981 (NEXIS).

See also:

"Other Reports and Comment on Poland," Telegraph Agency of the Soviet Union in Russian for Abroad and Moscow Home Service, 18 December 1981, *The British Broadcasting Corporation, Summary of World Broadcasts,* December 19, 1981.

119" 'Solidarity' Supplement 16 October 1981. Solidarity Congress Resolution, Programme Resolution of First National Congress," *British Broadcasting Corporation,* Summary of World Broadcasts, October 30, 1981.

120Gary Thatcher, "South Africa Bans Foreign Reporters from Troubled Black Townships," *The Christian Science Monitor,* June 18, 1980, p. 3.

121"Conspiracy. Dateline: Manila," *Reuters,* August 19, 1982 (NEXIS).

122*Ibid.*

123*Ibid.*

124*Ibid.*

CHAPTER TEN

Efforts to Control VCRs and Videocassettes

If information control is as critical to governments as their hundreds of years of obsessive control efforts would imply, then the VCR medium may indeed pose a serious threat. The efforts of even very restrictive governments to control VCRs and videocassettes do not appear commensurate with such "dangers." Nor do control efforts, when exerted, seem to have much effect on VCR and cassette distribution. Any bans placed on VCRs and videocassettes by governments to date appear to have been routinely ignored by citizens. The Islamic government of Iran, for instance, in an effort to rid the country of things Western, has even imposed the death sentence in cases of videocassette possession and vending, but this has availed it very little. The previously quoted USIA cable says:

> the Khomeini regime attempted to eliminate western influences on Iranian culture after the revolution seeing film, television and radio as both the principal offenders and the greatest avenues for cultural change. The regime hoped that with censorship and revised programming it could use these media to inculcate in people a greater revolutionary and Islamic spirit. From accounts provided us, however, this effort has largely failed . . . Shortwave radio broadcasts, cassette tape, and video cassette recorders have proved to be too much for the regime to cope with and western culture is maintaining its impact in Iran.[1]

Most of the Eastern European countries and the Soviet Union have taken formal steps aimed at regaining some control over what people are watching on videocassettes. They have declared their outrage and issued warnings to their people. They are also providing limited numbers of supposedly controllable VCRs, and small supplies of approved video cassette programming. No evidence has been seen that this has made the slightest dent (in fact, quite the contrary) in the smuggling of Japanese and Western VCRs and banned films.

Bulgaria was among the first to take action aimed at "doing something" about the VCR/cassette invasion. *Radio Free Europe Research,* reporting that the Bulgarians are very alarmed over the inroads being made by VCRs and videocassettes, says:

the unexpectedly triumphal march of the video revolution, despite the prohibitive prices involved, is seen as a very real threat to the regime's censorship. . . .[2]

The report describes steps the Bulgarians have taken to attempt to control them, first, in 1982, by setting up a state enterprise called Videofilm, attached to the Cinematography Trust. This organization

was supposed to meet educational, propagandistic, ideological, advertising, official, and private demands. Among other things, Videofilm was expected to exercise some sort of control over marketing. . . .[3]

This step was apparently ineffective. In 1984, the Bulgarian Video Association was established, under the chairmanship of Georgi Nakov, a party official highly experienced in organization with a master's degree in ideological propaganda. This appointment of "a cultural Tzar" who reports to a deputy prime minister indicates, a source for Eastern Europe says, the importance Bulgaria attaches to VCRs and cassettes and to getting control over them.[4] At the establishment of the new Association, Deputy Prime Minister Yordanov of the Committee on Culture, to whom the new Association reports, described its purpose as being

"to meet the pressing need to adopt and use video films and video programs" in all areas of culture and social life . . . [and] to plan and coordinate the production, importation, and exportation of video tapes, programs, equipment, and spare parts, and to manage all related matters.[5]

Yordanov is said to have emphasized that the prime purpose of the Association would be

"to enhance the role of the medium of video in our general cultural, educational, and political work." The association is supposed to be "a bridge to . . . [and] an effective ideological means of communist education."[6]

The Association reserves all rights to rent out private video equipment, and all cameras, recorders, or other video equipment, whether state owned or private, must be registered. Similar actions have now been taken by most Eastern European countries. In Poland, it is said that InterPress, the agency that maintains controls over foreign journalists, planned in spring 1985 to take over the whole business of VCR and videocassette rentals.[7] InterPress saw such a takeover, not only as a means to control an independent force, but also as a means of making money.[8] The money-making potential for whoever controls VCRs and cassettes in Eastern Europe has also been stressed by a personal contact. Czechoslovakia announced, in March 1985,

> that the government had approved a long-term program for the development of audiovisual equipment (including video recorders, cameras, and record players). . . .[9]

Deputy Prime Minister Jaromir Obzina of that country announced that the program would be involved in

> stepping up of the modest production of video recorders accomplished to date as well as the production and distribution of suitable programs on video cassettes. . . .[10]

Hungary was relatively slow to react to the VCR and videocassette invasion, but it also implemented a program in 1985 in which, it was said,

> special emphasis will be placed on the production and dissemination of Hungarian-made programs that will be "in harmony with the principles of (official) cultural policy."[11]

Like the rest of Eastern Europe, Hungary is unsure of success. *Radio Free Europe* concluded a report on Hungary by saying:

> While hoping that the various legal, economic, and administrative measures currently contemplated will be successful . . . [Hungary] also seems to have reluctantly accepted the fact that the video boom and the general communications revolution that it represents can no longer be brought under full control in the traditional totalitarian sense. In consequence, it has lowered its sights, and now would appear to be satisfied if it manages to keep ahead in a rapidly moving game. . . .[12]

According to a source for the German Democratic Republic,

> the authorities clearly intend to regulate acquisition or access to such equipment as carefully as they regulate access to all forms of information which can be controlled. VCR equipment is not available in the hard currency shops, even though the expense of such machines would guarantee only a few purchasers. Availability of VCRs for teaching purposes is tightly controlled. Some equipment is available for seminars or meetings through special offices staffed with video technicians who also maintain limited libraries of videotapes, mostly on educational subjects or tapes of GDR television programs . . . .[13]

Remarking on the limited numbers of VCRs in the country, this source also said that "GDR controls are pervasive and effective."[14] A source for Eastern

Europe has indicated however, that the GDR is following the same pattern of VCR penetration as the rest of the countries of Eastern Europe.

The KGB is said to be deeply concerned about VCRs, and the Russians are dead serious about controlling all information.[15] All information equipment in the USSR is closely controlled. Duplicating machines are not permitted privately, and, within the Ministries, they are locked up to prevent after-hours uses.[16] The KGB is very actively prosecuting Soviet officials who accept VCRs from foreign businessmen. In 1983, Andropov launched an anticorruption campaign which is still continuing. Because the VCR is so very desirable, it is high on the list of the items to be controlled. But its members still continue to grow and to circulate through the Russian black market.[17] Asked why the Soviets do not control VCRs and videocassettes more rigidly than they do, a source for the USSR said that the Soviets are ambivalent about this subject and about progress in general. They are always moving in two directions. In this case, the police want to control information, but the government wants to keep up with the rest of the world.[18]* Several sources indicate that, thus far, VCRs and cassettes are still relatively few in the USSR and may therefore still be tolerable. MIT Professor Loren Graham has said that videocassettes are still well down on the list of technologies for political uses.[20] But, in a mid-1984 article, *U.S. News and World Report* indicated that the KGB was thought to be creating a network of informers and taking other steps to control videocassettes. It said:

> for the time being, unapproved movies circulated in the VCR network reach only a few. But viewers are among the most influential and best-educated Soviet citizens, and some Westerners believe the effect of this tiny hole in the Iron Curtain eventually could be more far-reaching than anything imaginable today.[21]

The worry is obviously there in the Soviet Union, but just what will be done about it has not yet been clearly indicated. The Soviets' effort to create their own VCRs and programming is an attempt to gain some control, but as noted, this has been quite unsuccessful.[22]

Many countries have been making an effort to comply with copyright claims, some in response to U.S. pressure. The U.S. Congress has made trade benefit eligibility under the Caribbean Basin Economic Recovery Act dependent in part on more vigorous protection of U.S. intellectual prop-

---

* This conflict between the desire to keep up with the world and the desire to control information has also been mentioned by a source for the German Democratic Republic who says that GDR officials have a concern, "more or less openly expressed, that keeping up with the Western world as it moves toward becoming an information society might present problems for Communist institutions. . . ."[19]

erty.[23] The U.S. Executive branch has also been pressuring such countries as Taiwan, Singapore, and Korea to give better protection against video and other piracy.[24] Compliance by various countries often takes the form of anti-piracy raids, which pick up a few culprits or drive them from one base of operations to another. William Nix, Director of MPAA's antipiracy program, said in December 1984 that,

> in the first half of 1984, industry seized "more than 200,000 illegal cassettes, supervised over 2,000 investigations and obtained over 200 criminal convictions around the world."[25]

But, since this is just a drop in the bucket compared to the total global illegal activity, the end result is like a drug bust that hauls in a few pounds of cocaine or a few bales of marijuana. It leaves intact the basic structure of illegal conduits through which videocassettes are distributed globally.

While several nations have upped fines for piracy, several others, including Holland, just don't want the extra bureaucratic and police work. Stiffer penalties have been recommended in the Netherlands, but cases are tried in civil, not criminal, courts.[26] At least 50% of video cassettes in Holland were still pirated in 1984, and organized crime was specifically mentioned to be involved in this activity.[27]

Many countries have updated, and others are trying to update, their censorship laws to encompass videocassettes. Those who do so often find the workload to be overpowering. In Iceland, a country about the size of Kentucky, videocassettes come in by the "truckload."[28] In the nine months between February and October 1984, its Censorship Board had examined in excess of 2000 titles, with another 500 allowed to be marketed but still awaiting censorship clearance.[29] One problem is the sheer bulk involved. The New Zealand Customs Department, for instance, was pressed into service by that government to censor incoming videocassettes. These amounted to more than 11,000 tapes in a 12-month period.[30]

In Sri Lanka, there has been disagreement over who should be responsible for videocassettes. Legislation for the state-run television says that among Sri Lankan Rupa Vahini Corporation's duties are to "exercise supervision and control over the use of video cassettes and the production of programme material on such cassettes for export. . . ."[31] The chairman of the corporation, however, did not know how to go about implementing this, and, when he sought advice from the Ministry of State, who is charged with informational broadcasting, that Ministry is said to have disclaimed responsibility.

In Spain, all pre-recorded cassettes must be licensed, and that country is reportedly preparing a law both to crack down on piracy and to eliminate un-authorized viewing. But the Spaniards are not sanguine that this will make any practical difference. An *InterMedia* article expressed the opinion that

> most people will continue to behave as they always have done; the video clubs will duplicate more copies than they should; the distributors will declare to the treasury only half the number of copies they have actually sold; the video ad-dicts will continue to make their own copies; and the pirates will make and dis-tribute unauthorized recordings of popular films. . . .[32]

Malaysia has tightened up on censorship of videocassettes and has in-creased checks on VCR rental centers. Burma jails offenders. But the circu-lation of illegal videocassettes continues.[33]

Indonesia has made one of the most strenuous and sweeping efforts of any country to control videocassettes. Under Presidential Decision 13, in 1983, it has basically nationalized the video rental industry by authorizing only three state-owned companies to import, reproduce, or distribute any type of videocassette intended for use by individuals. Various documents concern-ing import, ownership, censorship, and intended use must be filed before these companies can take any action.[34] Under this legislation, only master copies are allowed in, and reproduction must be local. Prior to this new legis-lation, about 100 illegal distributors were operating, compared to eight offi-cial ones.[35] Various reports indicate that the success of the new effort has been limited.[36]

Regarding Asia in general, *Reuters* says: "Overwhelmed official censors complain they just cannot cope with millions of video cassettes flooding the Asian market. . . ."[37] Inadequate laws have also been cited, but where laws exist or are implemented, they have been unable to prevent the influx.

The Chinese government has, at least for the time being, moved away from the strenuous control of VCRs and cassettes that was attempted dur-ing the short-lived campaign against "spiritual pollution," for fear of jeopardizing its economic modernization by giving opportunities for general crackdowns to its more conservative opponents.

Regarding the failure of national governments to respond to the new chal-lenge being presented by videocassette recorders, Christine Ogan of the Indiana University School of Journalism says:

> wherever it surfaces, the discussion of policy change has focused on broadcast technology and content planned by, or under the supervision of government organizations. . . .[38]

But policymakers have not even addressed the problem of VCRs, although this is, she says, "The greatest potential threat to the total disintegration of national communication policy. . . ."[39] One reason, she says, is that the VCR is still considered a private medium, and not a medium for mass communications.

Professor Ogan remarked on the contradictory attitudes concerning VCRs in developing countries, saying:

> for Third World countries, it is curious that in the face of the strong stand taken on the New World Information Order, and the vehement attacks levelled against the West for usurping local cultural values with imported media, so little should be done to control this more insidious cultural invasion . . . other than establishing quotas or restricting imports to families who have lived abroad and brought back VCRs as a part of their household goods, I know of no country that has prevented VCR importation.[40]

The fact that there is, as yet, no really effective control over VCRs and cassettes in no way indicates that the desire of governments for information control has diminished. This study has uncovered no shortage of censorship of books, newspapers, radio, television — of whatever falls in the traditional framework or, especially, where the government controls the means of production and dissemination. This censorship ranges from mild to totally crippling. Haifaa Khalafallah, writing on the Middle Eastern situation, commented:

> it is hard to speak of conventional censorship in a state in which any alternative form of thinking is against the state laws and directly touches the security of the state. It is also hard to speak of censorship where the state owns and controls all the means of communication. In the Middle East, journalists, writers, actors, novelists, poets, news commentators, are often employees of the state. The interests of the community are watched over not by public opinion or the community consensus, but by soldiers. . . .[41]

Douglas Boyd explains how VCRs and videocassettes are shifting control over information from governments to their people:

> Among the many reasons that VCR ownership is increasing is that the machines are a means of gaining control over media consumption — a video equivalent of print material that is consumed at one's convenience. To some extent, the tapes are similar to books, but the consumer does not have to be literate to participate. VCRs are status symbols among all classes of people. The machines allow owners differing degrees of often forbidden fruit; pornography, banned political and religious material, uncensored western television programs, and feature films.[42]

VCRs, he says, are so popular that not even the Soviet Union, and certainly not any developing country, has the power to control them.

Part of the reason for lack of control has been described earlier, in the compromises made with the necessity for black markets, and the need to placate migrants. Part is that illegal activities in VCRs and cassettes got in on the ground floor and it will be difficult if not impossible for governments to shake them. Part is that the world's borders have largely become sieves, letting in, not only VCRs and cassettes, but also illegal drugs, arms, and migrants. Part is due to the conflicting desires within a given nation — the necessity for the government to grant the wishes of both the most conservative and the most liberal factions to maintain political equilibrium. Partly, as in China, major control has had to be sacrificed to allow economic modernization to continue. Partly, nations are kidding themselves. Poland, for instance, and other communist countries maintain the myth that they still control the monopoly on all programming. Partly, governments were caught by surprise by this new technology, and changing laws to cover it often runs into conflicts with other priorities.

Part of the reason for lack of control also appears to be that, in some countries, the worst has happened and it doesn't seem so bad after all. Videocassettes are the new opiate of the people, and, while they are watching them, they are not rioting.

That these various leniencies by governments may be shortsighted from their point of view is another story. *Rolling Stone* has said, in reference to VCRs,

> by the time England's infamous Luddites thought to destroy knitting machines, the Industrial Revolution had been going on for at least a hundred years, and their protests turned out to be more romantic fatalism than effective politics.[43]

But in many cases, governments believe they are doing all they can do, given the other demands they face.

NOTES

[1]"Censorship and Entertainment in Iran," Unclassified United States Information Agency cable, United States Department of State from U.S. Mission, Berlin, September 1985.

[2]"Bulgaria Goes Into the Video Business," Situation Report, Bulgaria/13, *Radio Free Europe Research,* Radio Free Europe-Radio Liberty, October 10, 1984, p. 4.

[3]*Ibid.*, p. 1.

[4]Eastern Europe. Personal communications.

G. S., "Bulgaria Goes Into the Video Business," Situation Report, Bulgaria/13, *Radio Free Europe Research,* Radio Free Europe-Radio Liberty, October 10, 1984., p. 2.

[5]G. S., "Bulgaria Goes Into The Video Business," Situation Report, Bulgaria/13, *Radio Free Europe Research,* Radio Free Europe-Radio Liberty, October 10, 1984, p. 2.

[6]*Ibid.,* p. 2.

[7]Douglas Stanglin. Personal communications.

[8]*Ibid.*

[9]V. S., "On the Verge of the Video Revolution," Situation Report, Czechoslovakia/9, *Radio Free Europe Research,* Radio Free Europe-Radio Liberty, June 3, 1985, p. 32.

[10]*Ibid.*

[11]Steven Koppany, "Unprepared Regime Scrambles to Meet Challenges of the Video Era," Situation Report, Hungary/10, *Radio Free Europe Research,* Radio Free Europe-Radio Liberty, September 4, 1985, p. 20.

[12]*Ibid.,* p. 21.

[13]German Democratic Republic. Personal communications.

[14]*Ibid.*

[15]The Soviet Union. Personal communications.

[16]*Ibid.,* and also:

Loren Graham, *Computers in the Soviet Union.* Program on Information Resources Policy Seminar, Harvard University, February 4, 1985.

Donald R. Shanor, *Behind the Lines. The Private War Against Soviet Censorship.* St. Martin's Press, New York, 1985.

[17]The Soviet Union. Personal communications.

[18]*Ibid.*

[19]German Democratic Republic. Personal communications.

[20]Loren Graham, *Computers in the Soviet Union,* Program on Information Resources Policy Seminar, Harvard University, February 4, 1985.

[21]"Out of Reach of the Curious Censors," *U.S. News & World Report,* July 23, 1984, p. 46.

[22]"VCRs That Will Spout The Party Line," *Business Week,* September 3, 1984, p. 40.

[23]David Ladd, "Latest Concern for Copyright Arouses Hopes," *Variety,* January 16, 1985, p. 1.

[24]*Ibid.,* and other sources.

[25]Richard Klein, "Pic Assn.'s Nix Gives Antipiracy Advice to Members of AFMA," *Variety,* December 12, 1984, p. 6.

[26]"Huffpuffing At Pirates By Video Trade Bodies Doesn't Do The Trick," *Variety,* October 17, 1984, p. 62.

[27]*Ibid.*

[28]"Icelandic Censors Under Full Steam," *Variety,* October 10, 1984, p. 112.

[29]*Ibid.*

[30]Mike Nicolaidi, "N.Z. Customs Dept. Wants to Lose Role as Product Censor," *Variety,* November 9, 1984, p. 47.

[31]Lasdanda Kurukulasuriya, "The Rich Relax With Imported Video," *InterMedia,* July/September 1983, p. 69.

[32]Diego A. Manrique, "Spain. The Third Channel," *InterMedia,* July/September, 1983, p. 68.

[33]Malaysia. Personal communications.

[34]Indonesia. Personal communications.

[35]Isabelle Reckeweg, "Dateline: Jakarta," *United Press International,* April 26, 1983 (NEXIS).

[36]Francis Daniel, "Dateline: Singapore," *Reuters,* September 24, 1983 (NEXIS).

[37]*Ibid.*

[38]Christine L. Ogan, "Media Diversity and Communications Policy. Impact of VCRs and Satellite TV," *Telecommunications Policy,* March 1985, p. 63.

[39]*Ibid.,* p. 64.

⁴⁰*Ibid.*, p. 68.

⁴¹Haifaa Khalafallah, "Closing the Door of Thought. The Background to Censorship of Contemporary Arabic Literature," *Index on Censorship,* June, 1984, p. 31.

⁴²Douglas A. Boyd, Speech, *Technology, Communication, and Development Theory: The Impact of the Home Video Cassette Recorder on Third World Countries,* speech, International Institute of Communications 1984 Annual Conference, Berlin, September 21-23, 1984, pp. 7-8.

See also:

Douglas A. Boyd and Joseph D. Straubhaar, "Developmental Impact of The Home Video Cassette Recorder on Third World Countries," *Journal of Broadcasting & Electronic Media,* Volume 29, Number 1, Winter 1985, pp. 9-10.

⁴³Kenneth Turan, "The Art of Revolution. Video is Taking Over Popular Culture," *Rolling Stone,* December 20, 1984/January 3, 1985, p. 75.

CHAPTER ELEVEN

Conclusions

When this study began, we were treated to large quantities of popular wisdom that said VCRs were too heavy and ungainly, and videocassettes too large, to conveniently smuggle; that customs would confiscate copier and copy; that languages and standards would be well nigh insurmountable; that only the elites could handle such sophisticated equipment, and only the rich could afford it. While these factors have undoubtedly been obstacles, this study has shown they have been no match for the legions bent on overcoming them. VCRs and videocassettes have deeply penetrated into even the major communist countries of Eastern Europe. While their numbers in the USSR are thought to be still limited, even there they are steadily growing. In Iran, VCRs and Western content on videocassettes are widely available despite a ban on both, and despite severe punishments and even death sentences. In Indonesia, notwithstanding the "nationalization" of VCRs and videocassettes, with the import and distribution limited to three government-controlled companies, more than 90% of all videocassettes are still illegally imported and distributed.

In country after country, specifically banned items — Indian films in Pakistan and Bangladesh, "Sadat" in Egypt, "Death of a Princess" in Saudi Arabia, Western films in Eastern Europe, and pronography everywhere — are readily available on videocassette, although kept out of cinemas and off television. Videocassettes and VCRs have penetrated even to small island nations and other countries bereft of television. They are providing TV substitutes, but without any of the governmental restrictions automatically placed on broadcasting.

Rapid and uniform introduction of VCRs and videocassettes into most nations has been greatly facilitated by the widespread existence of black market economies, the economic pressures exerted by migrant workers on their governments, and the early and vigorous entry of suppliers of pirated programming, including organized crime activities. Their ease of entry also indicates that extreme porosity of the world's borders exists from a wide variety of causes.

While people globally are mainly using VCRs and videocassettes for much desired entertainment, a great deal of what they watch their governments would prefer to ban or censor. Many groups are gathering in illegal settings to watch together what they are not permitted to watch in cinemas.

Individuals are also sometimes creating their own shows, and the political content, though still limited, seems to be growing.

Political acts perpetrated via VCRs and videocassettes have not so far appeared to be numerous, but a variety of such acts have been committed. Videocassettes have been used for propaganda in guerrilla warfare in El Salvador; by the Philippine people to overcome government suppression of information during a political crisis; by Lebanese suicide bombers to leave inspirational messages, and in the U.S. and South Africa to transmit antisemitic sentiments, among various other examples. There is no technical obstacle to such political implementation of VCRs and cassettes, given the desire to so use them.

While the concerns expressed overtly by governments have so far been for the most part mild and often vague, governments are definitely worried about the political potential of video technologies. The major communist countries are afraid that they might be used for samizdat. Indonesia is afraid they might spread subversive messages from China. Malaysia is worried that they might be used by the fundamentalist Islamic minority against the modernization efforts of the Islamic majority. Saudi Arabia is worried that its lack of control over content offensive to the country's most conservative factions might weaken the power of government. Many countries are afraid of cultural erosion. Many countries are afraid people will tune out broadcast TV in favor of VCRs, thus robbing the government of the ability to use television to get across its own messages. Neighbors have begun to worry about the political antics of neighbors on television for fear they will be taped and distributed in their own countries. In at least two instances—India after the assassination of Indira Ghandi, and Saudi Arabia at the showing in many nations of the television docudrama, "Death of a Princess"—governments have strenuously objected to and/or tried to control the television of others.

While a number of countries have instituted some type of control over VCRs and cassettes, and many have other media controls that could be expected to apply here, nowhere—and this includes the major communist countries—have these controls been seen to be effective. There appear to be a variety of reasons for this. It has been seen that, in China, an "open door" policy to promote economic growth and modernization has been given deliberate precedence over control of the "spiritual pollution" brought in by foreign content. It has been seen that, in countries heavily dependent on migrant remittances, VCRs must be allowed in to placate those migrant workers. Many countries rely for economic viability on highly advanced black market systems which offer illegal conduits for distributing VCRs and videocassettes, both across national borders and internally. In Iran, the government owes revolutionary debts to the bazaars and needs their support to continue existence.

In short, a powerful economic consideration often stays the government from cracking down politically. There are also conflicting political considerations, of course, including the need to maintain an equilibrium between the varying wishes of different factions of a given country. The wishes for modernization vs. the wish to retain traditions seen in Moslem countries, and the desire of communist countries to control information vs. the desire to keep up with the West technologically, are two such instances.

It would seem that VCRs and videocassettes are in most countries to stay, and everything indicates they will increase in numbers. VCRs are following the course set by audiocassettes — as conduits for political information as well as entertainment. In countries such as the USSR, where "printing press" is the buzzword implying political activity, videocassettes may, at least for awhile, play a role that is somewhat subordinate to the print media. In Third World countries, however, where printing is rarer and reading ability is limited, those politically inclined are likely to jump to the new technology with great facility. Developing nations have already done this in such areas as air transport and satellite communications. Videocassettes supply the immediacy of television without its political impediments. Political messages can thus be easily distributed in this form of uncensored mass visual entertainment.

VCRs and videocassettes are not necessarily more destabilizing than older technologies, but neither need they be any less so. They are the latest fad and status symbol, which could mean they make more of an impact than more familiar older media. They have put a wider range of materials in the hands of individuals than has ever before happened. VCRs and videocassettes are democratizing by the fact that they make information available to illiterate people. They are democratizing in that they give the individual whatever information is wanted. While their expense at this time confines them somewhat to elites, this study has shown that, through import by migrant workers, through group showings in homes, through village square viewings, through video parlors offering cinema substitutes for pennies, and through cheap rental fees, videocassette programming is quickly being extended to large groups of non-affluent people.

Walter Wriston, former Chairman of CitiCorp, has said, concerning information technologies in general, "History teaches that change occurs when people learn there is an alternative to what they believed to be their lot in life."[1] The rapid global spread of VCRs and videocassettes cannot fail to apprise the world's people of alternate ways of doing things. The very act of acquiring access to VCRs and videocassettes, despite their governments' inclinations, gives people a major alternative. This alternative has not been worked for by individuals, but is a gift of accident, like an unexpected legacy. A big question is, will individuals realize the potency of these new controls, and, in the end, will they be able to hang onto them? The capabilities of

VCRs and videocassettes have hardly begun to be tested. What can be done with them, given determination and ingenuity, still remains to be seen.

So far as the future is concerned, we are only left with questions:

Will countries be forced to improve their television markedly to remain in competition?

Will the increased use of VCRs and cassettes tend to leave politics and international affairs to smaller and smaller groups in restrictive countries? Will it open new opportunities? Will it narrow the group of active political participants in the democracies, as audiences withdraw from news and commentary to watch a steady diet of movies?

How deep will the social and cultural implications be of these new sources of mass information?

How much are VCRs and cassettes likely to be used for propagandizing, destabilizing, or terrorizing? What is their potential for advancing a specific propaganda objective, say by mass production and widespread — even worldwide — distribution? Are they potential tools for artificially created material for use as deliberate, masterplan projects of disinformation?

If VCRs should usurp governmental and mass media control, will this make for global harmony or divisiveness? Would their spread of literacy and technology compensate for possible damages to cultures and societies?

Will the never-never-land of the VCR movie lure increasingly more illegal immigrants across world borders? If so, what will be, on balance, the likely political benefits and prices?

Is the access to VCR/cassette information and products a new way to redistribute global resources? Will battles to retain traditional control over copyright lead to new international systems or tensions?

What does it do to the legitimacy of governments for masses of people to be able to and actually routinely flaunt their orders? What, in the long term, will be the consequences of such widespread civil disobedience?

Are debates over DBS (direct broadcasting by satellite) passe? Have all the arguments in UNESCO, assuming state control over information, now become day-before-yesterday's issues?

NOTES

[1]Walter Wriston, *Microseconds and Macropolicy*, speech, American Enterprise Institute, December 6, 1984.

Personal Communications Concerning the Political Consequences of the Global Spread of VCRs and Videocassettes

The following information has been extracted from the answers received by the authors in personal communications with a number of contacts concerning countries in various parts of the world. As described in the introduction, to permit frankness in answering, anonymity was assured. All contacts were Americans, and all either were resident in, travel frequently to, or are otherwise thoroughly familiar with the involved country. Information was provided for the following 30 countries and one geographic area: Bangladesh, Brazil, Colombia, Czechoslovakia, Eastern Europe as a whole, El Salvador, East Germany (GDR), Ecuador, Egypt, Hong Kong, India, Indonesia, Israel, Jordan, Kenya, South Korea, Malaysia, Nepal, Nigeria, Pakistan, Panama, Philippines, Saudi Arabia, Somalia, South Africa, Thailand, Turkey, USSR, Yugoslavia, Zaire, and Zimbabwe.

Most of the contacts answered or used as guidance a questionnaire containing the following questions (although not all people could answer all questions):

1. Is there any evidence that VCRs and their programming are being put to any underground use in (your country)?
2. Is there any indication of their use thus far for purposes that might be construed as subversive? Could you comment on the potential for such use?
3. Does the government seem nervous about this availability to private citizens? If so, has it done, or does it threaten to do anything about it?
4. Has the government itself made use of VCRs and cassettes to spread misinformation or propaganda?
5. Is there any history of the use of audiotapes for the above political purposes in your country?
6. What percentage of the people in your country have access to television and of these, how many would you estimate have VCRs?

A few contacts were asked to answer a specific question, or to give more sweeping opinions of the overall VCR or videocassette situation in a given country. These answers have been discussed in the body of this paper, and will not be repeated here.

Question 1.   Is There Any Evidence That VCRs and Their Programming Are Being Put to Any Underground Use in (Your Country)?

Bangladesh: "In a sense. Illegal VCRs of Indian movies which are not allowed in Bangladesh, and uncensored western films, some of which may be pornographic by even western standards, are freely available and widely watched in Bangladesh. Many video clubs for rentals and illegal video parlors exist and private ownership of VCRs is very widespread among families that can afford them."

Brazil: "No."

Colombia: "It is impossible . . . to comment accurately on any subversive, underground, propagandistic or political use of videotape materials . . . without exhaustive research. . . . This is not a problem, however, which comes up in the normal course of conversation with Colombians. . . . Colombia is a nation which adheres to the same democratic principles of free speech and free flow of information as the United States."

Czechoslovakia; "No."

German Democratic Republic: "Although there is no evidence that VCRs or their programming are being used surreptitiously or for any purposes that might be construed as subversive, the authorities clearly intend to regulate acquisitions or access to such equipment as carefully as they regulate access to all forms of information which can be controlled. VCR equipment is not available in the hard currency shops, even though the expense of such machines would guarantee only a few purchasers. Availability of VCRs for teaching purposes is tightly controlled. Some equipment is available for seminars or meetings through special offices staffed with video technicians who also maintain limited libraries of videotapes, mostly on educational subjects or tapes of GDR television programs. Even film makers have complained that one of the obstacles they face when they try to sell their films abroad is the difficulty in making videotapes of their works. 'We lack the equipment in this country to make tapes of all of our films. But foreign distributors don't screen films before buying them any more — they just want you to leave your tape. . . .' [said one]."

This contact adds that there is a more or less openly expressed concern by GDR leaders that "keeping up with the Western world as it moves toward be-

coming an information society might present problems for Communist institutions. . . ."

Ecuador: "None, if one defines 'underground' in a political sense. There is, of
course, widespread violation of U.S. copyrights."

Egypt: "No."

Hong Kong: "No."

India: "No discernable evidence that this is being done. . . ."

Indonesia: There is an active black market in uncensored imported
videotapes—first-run feature films and pornography. The government is
trying to put a stop to the black market, but many elite audiences are quite
matter-of-fact about the "door-to-door" video rental salesmen who arrive on
a motorcycle with a black briefcase full of 50–75 titles, mostly abysmal in
quality of reproduction—but of popular and relatively new films."

Israel: "No."

Jordan: "No."

Kenya: "I have noted no attempts yet to use videos for political purposes. On
the contrary, I would think owners now rarely tune in television—where the
President can be seen nightly on the news—in favor of watching American
films. How this shapes their image of America interests me, but I have no
wisdom to offer on the subject." . . . "The Government of Kenya would like
to find a way to tap this potential revenue source, but other than levying
heavy duties on recorders, they have not yet found it. Virtually all the
videotapes are bootlegged from British screens and appear within days after
having been seen there. The bootlegging network is awesome, to say the
least."

South Korea: "Underground VCRs consist of pornography which is tightly
controlled by the Government and feature films which have not yet received
permission to be shown in Korean commercial theatres."

Malaysia: "No."

Nepal: " No."

Nigeria: "Video cassette tapes are sold on the street by vendors but no 'underground' use [is] evident."

Pakistan: "There is no evidence that VCRs are being put to any underground use in Pakistan for political purposes."

Panama: "No . . . there is extensive use of VCRs in Panama, but [there is]
no reason to believe that they are being used for any purpose but entertain-

ment and, to a lesser extent, education. Most of the material available consists of movies and other shows of that type."

Saudi Arabia: "I am unaware of any underground use of VCRs in Saudi Arabia. TV and VCRs are a big thing in the Kingdom, much more widespread than in any [other] country [I know of]. Ubiquitous is an apt description. But they just are not used, from all that I know, for the purposes your questions seem to imply. . . ."

Somalia: "No, although pirated versions of video programs are available at video shops in Mogadishu. [I would] estimate that Mogadishu has approximately 100 video rental shops, a remarkable number in view of the size of the city and its economic condition."

South Africa: "I have never seen a press story or other source pointing to 'underground' use of VCR's. There are, of course, in this inhibited society reports of seizures of pornographic tapes or so called blue movies.' "

Thailand: "Their use is not illegal here. However, the use of pirated, commercially produced programs from other countries is spreading rapidly. Many of these would not pass govt. censors if submitted for media use even though the Thai media is relatively unrestricted by world standards."

Turkey: "No."

Yugoslavia: ". . . Yugoslavia is basically quite an open society. The role of the VCR here approaches what it is in Western Europe: a form of entertainment that will soon become a basic item, like the television set itself, in the more affluent home."

Zimbabwe: "There is no evidence that VCR's have been put to any underground use in Zimbabwe."

Question 2.   Is There Any Indication of Their Use Thus Far for Purposes That Might Be Construed As Subversive? Could You Comment On The Potential for Such Use?

Bangladesh: "There is no known subversive use of VCRs in Bangladesh to date and I see little potential for it under present political conditions. The present government, although a Martial Law regime, allows a fairly high degree of freedom of information and subversion by VCR would not appear necessary in Bangladesh."

Brazil: "No. The potential at this time is unknown."

Czechoslovakia: "Videotapes of Western films, both standard fare and pornography, are widely circulated, copied illegally, and even rented — all outside the regular channels of state control."

German Democratic Republic: "One could argue whether this lack of availability (mentioned in Question 1) is the result of a specific fear of subversion through videocassettes, of concern about the effect of access to any medium or the result of insufficient hard currency resources to purchase such expensive equipment. After all, television from West Germany is available to eighty per cent of the homes of GDR citizens, and the GDR government is even laying cable to reach those areas of the country which could not receive West German programming because of geographical barriers. On the other hand, the very ready availability of source broadcasts from the FRG could be seen as a threat by GDR authorities. It is an increased risk, perhaps, to be able to save programs and to screen them later with like-minded friends or with a circle of dissidents. . . ."

Ecuador: "None. While there would be some audience for VCR materials, indications thus far are that those few individuals engaged in subversive activities here are still operating at the smudgy handbill and anonymous telephone call level."

Egypt: "No."

Hong Kong: "None; and, given the access to and availability of information in Hong Kong, there would seem to be little potential for such use."

India: "There is no indication that such use is in effect. Since the trend in India indicates a slow and moderate build-up of privately owned VHS equipment, any enterprising individual could engage in such activity on a limited, selective basis; however, since the Government is focusing on the illegal importation of VCRs and VCR piracy, any software may be liable to close scrutiny. . . ."

Indonesia: [I am] not aware of any 'subversive' use in the Western sense of the term. However, the Government of Indonesia takes a strict view of the "undesirable influences" (Presidential Decision 13, 1983) of imported videotapes. One example, the relatively innocuous film, "The Year of Living Dangerously" (which has not played in Indonesian theaters) circulated widely in the VTR black market."

Israel: "No. Israel being a free and open society, there are so many other possibilities and channels that it doesn't apply. The potential would seem to exist in the occupied territories, however . . . no evidence [has been seen] of their use."

Jordan: "No. However, such potential exists. Despite strict censorship and checking, videotapes can be easily smuggled in."

South Korea: "No."

Malaysia: "No."

Nepal: "No."

Nigeria: "No indication at all."

Pakistan: "No."

Panama: "No."

Somalia: "No."

South Africa: "I see no indication that VCR's are needed to get some elements of the populace angrier at the social system than they already are. In the kinds of opposition seen at present, there is no type that is more easily taught by television than by any other means, e.g., demonstrations, strikes, letters to newspapers, etc."

Thailand: "I have heard of no such use for political ends although someone, somewhere probably has a 'subversive' tape or two."

Turkey: "No. Practically nonexistent."

Zimbabwe: "There is no indication that any party or group has to date used videos for any purpose that can be construed as subversive. On the other hand, there has been at least one video produced for television by a private producer . . . which was rejected by the Government Censorship Board. This particular production dealt with a political theme, was set in Ethiopia, but clearly could have been interpreted by Zimbabwean viewers as a statement on certain conditions in this country."

Question 3.   Does The Government Seem Nervous about This Availability to Private Citizens? If So, Has It Done, Or Does It Threaten to Do Anything about It?

Bangladesh: "Only in the moral and protectionist sense. Authorities periodically raid video parlors, seizing illegal Indian tapes, pornography, and the equipment of operators. Otherwise, only general exhortations about protecting the morals of the people and the local film industry are heard from time to time."

Brazil: "No."

Colombia: ". . . There is apparently no official effort to control video material . . . which has obviously been pirated. . . . however, . . . television programmers who rebroadcast material are careful to secure whatever rights are necessary as required by Colombian and international law."

Czechoslovakia: "There is an appreciation of the potential for 'subversion' on the part of Czechoslovak authorities but it does not appear that they are ready or able to institute measures to curb the use of VCRs or videocassettes. A lively black market in video cassettes and pirated materials exists in Prague, Bratislava (capital of Slovakia) and other major cities."

German Democratic Republic: ". . . GDR officials would be concerned by the uncontrollable aspect of VCR dissemination of knowledge. They learned that they could not stop people from watching FRG television, but are not likely to give up control of the dissemination of VCRs if they can avoid it."

Ecuador: "No. Pirated VCRs circulate freely through commercial clubs. There is no evidence of serious governmental concern."

Egypt: "No."

Hong Kong: "No."

India: "The [government of India] does not show any nervousness, at this point, about availability of software of all kinds to private citizens. It does, however, keep an eye on products provided by other governments. . . ."

Indonesia: "The government is definitely concerned about the VCR explosion, and especially about the underground black market in uncensored tapes. It has in effect 'nationalized' the video rental industry by insisting that only three specified state-owned facilities are authorized to reproduce videotapes of any kind, and then only after being presented with proper documents concerning importations, ownership, censorship clearance, and intended use. . . ."

Israel: "No. Only in the following instances: a). Unless it is damaging to the security of the state, it will be overlooked. b). The economic element is a factor the government is nervous about. The import of VCRs is being restricted for at least six months and it will be hard to control it. c). Porno VCRs are smuggled in. If shown in private homes, it is overlooked. Officially it is banned."

Jordan: "No, considering the numerous commercial video outlets available."

Kenya: ". . . VCRs are changing the entertainment habits of the wealthy residents, but there is no sign of their being put to political use. Nor is there any attempt to restrict access, other than general Government warnings against the distribution of pornography. Kenya is basically a free enterprise society and videotapes are a growth industry dominated largely by Asians."

South Korea: "The Government has made periodic efforts to stop the showings of pornographic VCRs particularly in public places such as coffee shops. These efforts will continue."

Malaysia: "The ready access to VCR recorders and tapes is a cause of government concern regarding undesirable elements of Western culture and possible communist ideological influences. Although the government is not unduly nervous about this, it has instituted tighter checks on VCR rental centers and increased exercise of official censorship of VCRs."

Nepal: "No."

Nigeria: "There is no control of VCR distribution."

Pakistan: "It seems that the government is nervous about VCRs availability to private citizens. Recently, it issued an order that a license would be required for possessing a VCR. The government's main concern is to check illegal showing of banned feature films and immoral movies."

Saudi Arabia: "I have not sensed any such nervousness."

Somalia: "No."

South Africa: "I would strongly doubt they are nervous. VCR's are available to anyone with 500 dollars (U.S.) to spend."

Thailand: "The government has periodically tried to control distribution of the pirated versions (almost all in circulation) in order to comply with copyright agreements. There is also discussion in the media of the long term effect of the heavy exposure to foreign culture. TV has been used as a carefully controlled unifier and purveyor of Thai culture. The VCR counteracts this influence."

Turkey: "No. Business is booming in Turkey."

Zimbabwe: "The Government applies the same censorship regulations on videos as it does on films. The rapid spread of video playback equipment in this country has created some concern, but Government censors and officials are primarily worried about the importation of pornographic material."

Question 4. Has the Government Itself Made Use of VCRs and Cassettes to Spread Misinformation or Propaganda?

Bangladesh: "Bangladesh has ambitious, two-channel color broadcasting on television, using many imported, especially U.S. products; e.g. Dallas, Dynasty, Charlie's Angels, MASH, children's programs and cartoons, Little

House on the Prairie, etc.; but [there is no known] use by the Government of propaganda or misinformation."

Brazil: "Not that I know of."

Czechoslovakia: "Certain Western programming which reinforces official policies have been used domestically on videocassettes; e.g., 'The Day After.' Upper level and privileged party officials are often 'rewarded' with access to Western video materials; i.e., Hollywood films or other entertainment vehicles."

German Democratic Republic: "[To my knowledge] the GDR has not made use of videocassetes or audiotapes to spread propaganda."

Ecuador: "No."

Egypt: "No ."

Hong Kong: "No."

India: "Yes, sources have indicated that the government of India has produced VCRs supporting its stand on the Punjab issue and the Indian Army's attack on the Golden Temple. These programs were given to many Congress-I leaders and diplomats leaving for overseas assignments with instructions that Indian Embassies abroad are to show these to selected target audiences of overseas Indians (especially Sikhs)."

Indonesia: "Not to my knowledge."

Israel: "No."

Jordan: "No.''

South Korea: "[I am] not aware of this activity."

Malaysia: "To the best of my knowledge, the government has not made use of VCRs or cassettes to spread misinformation or propaganda. The government does make active use of its government-owned television channels to disseminate government messages with themes that usually promote national integration, citizenship and items of educational value. The private television channel does on occasion, carry public service messages."

Nepal: "No."

Nigeria: "No."

Pakistan: "No."

Saudi Arabia: "No."

Somalia: "No."

South Africa: "There are firms which sell advertising as movie trailers on commercially rented movies and other cassettes. So there is some 'commercial propaganda'. I have never seen examples of government mis-information by VCR cassette."

Thailand: "No."

Turkey: "Tapes on the burgeoning market are screened very loosely by government censors, but there are no indications that the government itself is producing tapes for home consumption. . . . Not to my knowledge."

Zimbabwe: "The Government, except for Zimbabwe Television, has not acquired very much of a VCR capability. The major use of VCRs and cassettes is the Agritex department of the Ministry of Agriculture which uses the medium extensively for agricultural training in rural areas. The Ministry of Information has no VCR capability at this time."

Question 5.   Is There Any History of the Use of Audiotapes for the Above Political Purposes in Your Country?

Bangladesh: "No known use."

Brazil: "No knowledge of such a history."

Czechoslovakia: "There has been no significant use of audio tapes on the part of the government to spread misinformation or propaganda in recent years. This is probably due to the fact that the government controls all media, including more effective tools than audio cassettes."

Ecuador: "No."

Egypt: "Yes."

Hong Kong: "No."

India: "Yes, as cited above." (Question 4).

Indonesia: "Not to my knowledge, although polemical poetry is common here, and may well be circulated in audiotape format when it is too critical for public reading."

Israel: "No. If there is any, it is so minor that it is insignificant."

Jordan: "No."

South Korea: "[I am] not aware of this activity."

Malaysia: "No."

Nepal: "No."

Nigeria: "No."

Pakistan: "No."

Panama: "No."

Saudi Arabia: "To my knowledge, no."

Somalia: "No."

South Africa: "None that I am aware of."

Thailand: "Occasionally, audio-tapes of one political personality or another have been hawked by street vendors. The impact has been neglibible — rarely, if ever, mentioned in the free wheeling Bangkok press.

Turkey: "Not to my knowledge."

Zimbabwe: "No."

One of the contacts made the comment: "I understand, with absolutely no further knowledge, that cassettes have been used in the Seychelles by political dissidents. . . ."

Question 6. What Percentage of the People in Your Country Have Access to Television and of These, How Many Would You Estimate Have VCRs?

Bangladesh: "Out of 100 million Bangladeshis, only about two percent have access to television. About 0.75 percent of these have VCRs. These percentages are increasing rapidly, however, as travelers bring back machines, especially workers returning from the Gulf States."

Brazil: "Access: Approximately 77 million viewers see television. No data on ownership of VTRs."

Colombia: "As you may be aware, lending of Betamax videocassettes of material recorded in the United States and elsewhere for entertainment use is a big business in Colombia. The Betamax lending stores are located primarily in urban areas and taken advantage of by those wealthy enough to own videocassette recorders. . ." . . . "In a country with an estimated population of 29 million, about 15 million people have access to television. There are about 500 thousand videocassette recorders in Colombia."

Czechoslovakia: "Ninety-five percent plus of the population have access to television. I estimate fewer than 2,000 households have VCRs."

German Democratic Republic: ". . . According to the latest available figures (UNESCO, 1982) there are 342 television sets for each 1,000 people in the GDR. In effect, every individual in the GDR has access to a television set. I know of only a few individuals with a VCR, but have heard that several individuals in the entertainment or film fields have purchased such machines during foreign trips for home use. I would be surprised if there were more than a few hundred, however; GDR controls are pervasive and effective."

Ecuador: "Gallup of Ecuador indicates that 84% of city dwellers and 46 of those living in rural areas have access to television. They also estimate that 18% of the homes in the city of Quito have VCR equipment. I would estimate that the city of Guayaquil, the country's other major urban center, has at least that percentage and possibly more."

Egypt: "10% have access. [VCRs] 2%."

Hong Kong: "The Hong Kong Government estimates that 93 percent of households own one or more television sets. The number of VCRs is harder to estimate, but . . . one family in five owning a VCR is a reasonable guess."

India: "Ten percent of India's people have TV sets in their homes and an even greater percentage have access to TV through relatives, friends or community television sets. These figures will increase in the future because of the [government's] transmitter expansion program (by year's end [1984] there will be 180 transmitter sites). The goal of this expansion program is to provide 85 percent of India's population with access to TV. Less than 100,000 Indian families possess VCR's (mainly VHS format)."

Indonesia: "The following figures are current in the advertising industry in Indonesia, and are based on random sample research within the last six months [1984]. Number of TV sets in Indonesia: Color: 1,154,000. Black and White: 3,927,000. Percentage of adult Jakarta* respondents who:

Have a color TV at home: 21%
Have a black and white TV at home: 51%
Have a VCR at home: 7%
Watched TV yesterday: 54%
Have ever watched TV: 93%
Have ever watched a video cassette: 55%

---

* "Note that these figures cannot be extrapolated nationwide. Jakarta is the seat of virtually all government and financial activity, and the home of the large majority of the 'elite' population of the country."

Estimate of nationwide urban area viewers who are watching television during prime time (9:00 pm): 25–30%. (Urban residents comprise roughly 20% of the population of 160 million. However, surprisingly high numbers of rural people have access to television through a government program to place televisions in village squares for community use.)"

Israel: "TV = 95% VCR = 20% (based on population of four million)."

Jordan: "At least 90 percent of the Jordanian population have TV sets (or more than one set). I estimate about 15–20 percent of those who own TV sets also own VCR's."

Kenya: "VCRs are, as you have been told, extraordinarily popular here. The owners are mainly members of the European and Asian communities, with a sprinkling of wealthier Africans. Videotape shops have sprung up like mushrooms in the major cities. . . . The impact has been so great, particularly among film-loving Asians, that at least one major movie theater has closed in Nairobi. It is not unusual to see a sari-clad Asian woman carting a dozen or so videos to her car for a weekend's viewing. . . ."

South Korea: "About 97% of Korean households have television sets. VCR players are a major Korean export item and are available for domestic purchase at prices that are still considered expensive. [I] would estimate no more than 10% have VCRs."

Malaysia: "It is estimated that 93% of adults (over 15 years old) have access to television. Homes with television sets are estimated at 75%. 14% of the adult population have VCRs in their homes, ⅔ of them in the urban commercial centers."

Nepal: "There is no TV in Nepal, however, its introduction in the near future (within 2–3 years) is possible. There are estimated about 1,000–1,500 VCR's in Nepal. The recent lowering of duty on VCR's is likely to cause a rise in this number."

Nigeria: "22 million TV sets reported (population is 100 million); video recorders [are] owned by small percentage of elite. Cassette recorders [are] very expensive."

Pakistan: "According to the Pakistan Economic Survey, there are 760,000 licensed TV sets in Pakistan, i.e., about 1/10 of the population owns TV sets. There are five major TV broadcast stations, and their programs can be seen in all parts of the country. However, no figure is available about VCRs. TV and VCRs can be rented on nominal charges, therefore even the lowest group income people have access to them."

Panama: "80% own or have access to television. I estimate that 40,000 to 50,000 homes may have VCRs."

Saudi Arabia: "There are 5 to 8 million Saudis, depending on whose figures you accept, plus roughly another 3 million foreigners. Over 90 percent of the country is now covered by television and soon it will be 100 percent. VCRs are extremely popular, particularly, but not exclusively, in the cities. I would estimate totals of nearly 4 million TV sets and over 1 million VCRs, but reliable figures are not available."

Somalia: "It is difficult to give a percentage. Television was officially introduced in October, 1983. Until then, the elite and upper middle class relied on VCRs for television programming. A large number of VCRs and TVs have been imported by Somalis working in Saudi Arabia, Kuwait and the Arab Emirates as a form of repatriating their earnings to their families. Videos remain extremely popular."

South Africa:	Population Group	Access to TV	Ownership of VCR
	White	100%	84%
	Colored	80%	71%
	Indian	85%	48%
	African	50%	02%

Thailand: "60% + have access to TV. The number with VCR's or access to VCR's is probably still well within 5% but is growing very rapidly— 50–80% per year."

Turkey: "Turkish Radio and Television (TRT) calculates that there are over six million television sets in the country. Considering somewhat arbitrarily that an average of 5 persons use a single set, I estimate a potential audience of 30 million Turkish viewers. No one knows for certain, but commentators estimate that there are between one and two million VCR's in use in Turkey. There are more than 5,000 video clubs providing tapes to this audience at present."

Yugoslavia: "There are an estimated 4,200,000 television sets in the country. This means that there is a TV set for every three or four people. There are also an estimated 350,000 video recorders in Yugoslavia. Until recently, Yugoslavs could not import television sets. The purpose of this ban was to protect domestic production. Although VCRs were not produced in Yugoslavia, nor were they specifically prohibited from import under the law affecting TV sets, customs officials treated both VCRs and personal computers as if they were and excluded them from importation on the basis of the TV law and on the grounds that their value exceeded 5,000 new dinars, the value limit on goods Yugoslavs could import. Yugoslavs who work as

Gastarbeiters abroad were, however, permitted to import TVs and VCRs. The laws affecting what Yugoslavs can bring into the country are currently being revised. When they go into force, each Yugoslav traveler will be allowed to import one VCR. This means that the number of sets will proliferate even more. As far as cassettes themselves are concerned, the most recent American films, like 'Gorky Park', 'Indiana Jones and the Temple of Doom', are in wide circulation. I am told there is a big underground market in pornography as well."

Zaire: The source for Zaire mentioned that the "university types" were too poor to own VCRs but that some people in the mining companies had them.

Zimbabwe: "At the end of 1983 it was estimated that there were 84,000 television viewers in Zimbabwe (TV sets are licensed). On that basis it was estimated that 350,000 to 400,000 Zimbabweans view television at least once a week. It is estimated that there are 2,000 VCR machines in the country."

APPENDIX B

Penetration Figures

Figure 1. Broadcast Signal and VCR Distribution for All Countries as of December 31, 1983

Name of Country	TV Sets in Use*	Networks or Equiv.*	Exported VCRs**	VCRs as % of TV Sets†
Afghanistan	12,000	1	6,330	52.75
Albania	7,000	1	n/a	.00
Algeria	1,140,000	1	1,324	.12
Angola	21,000	1	132	.63
Antigua	9,300	1	n/a	.00
Arab Rep. of Egypt	3,850,000	2	40,290	1.05
Argentina	6,000,000	1	43,648	.73
Australia	5,500,000	2	1,462,168	26.58
Austria	2,477,000	2	42,231	1.70
Bahamas	50,000	1	156	.31
Bahrain	120,000	2	61,544	51.29
Bangladesh	178,975	1	218	.12
Barbados	48,000	1	146	.30
Belgium	2,976,383	2	257,697	8.66
Belize	12,000	n/a	n/a	.00
Benin	6,000	1	625	10.42
Bermuda	20,000	1	981	4.91
Bolivia	100,000	2	236	.24
Brazil	22,000,000	5	86,893	.39
British Virgin Islands	1,300	1	n/a	.00
Brunei	30,000	2	n/a	.00
Bulgaria	1,900,000	2	3,684	.19
Cambodia	30,000	1	n/a	.00
Cameron	n/a	n/a	1,910	.00
Canada	8,480,000	6	1,426,546	16.82
Central African Republic	100	1	n/a	.00
Chile	1,325,000	4	27,739	2.09
China	16,000,000	3	25,885	.16
China (Taiwan Province)	5,060,000	3	337,888	6.68
Colombia	1,750,000	3	1,515	.09
Congo	2,700	1	785	29.07

continued

Figure 1. (*Continued*)

Name of Country	TV Sets in Use*	Networks or Equiv.*	Exported VCRs**	VCRs as % of TV Sets†
Cook Islands	n/a	n/a	94	.00
Costa Rica	300,000	4	924	.30
Cuba	700,000	2	1,673	.24
Cyprus	110,000	1	149,828	136.21
Czechoslovakia	8,514,000	2	922	.01
Denmark	1,886,500	1	144,740	7.67
Djibouti	8,000	1	2,386	29.83
Dominican Republic	305,000	1	n/a	.00
East Germany	5,800,000	2	966	.02
Ecuador	500,000	4	3,394	.68
El Salvador	400,000	5	143	.04
Equatorial Guinea	500	1	n/a	.00
Ethiopia	45,000	1	23	.05
Fiji	n/a	n/a	16,892	.00
Finland	1,613,000	2	150,941	9.36
France	21,515,000	3	1,470,078	6.83
French Guiana	181,500	1	553	.30
French Polynesia	181,500	1	n/a	.00
Gabon	5,000	1	3,316	66.32
Ghana	70,000	1	52	.07
Gibraltar	7,100	1	4,605	64.86
Greece	1,700,000	1	87,776	5.16
Guam	n/a	n/a	14.177	.00
Guatemala	200,000	3	1,058	.53
Guyana	n/a	n/a	11	.00
Haiti	13,000	3	n/a	.00
Honduras	48,000	3	n/a	.00
Hong Kong	1,226,000	4	618,447	50.44
Hungary	2,900,000	2	1,712	.06
Iceland	62,600	1	1,914	3.06
India	2,095,537	5	76,765	3.66
Indonesia	1,250,000	1	52,149	4.17
Iran	2,000,000	2	7,167	.36
Iraq	500,000	1	48,780	9.76
Ireland	719,000	2	32,614	4.54
Israel	1,100,000	2	175,055	15.91
Italy	13,645,043	7	155,891	1.14
Ivory Coast	205,000	1	6,691	3.26
Jamaica	167,000	1	141	.08
Japan	30,403,046	3	n/a	.00
Jordan	200,000	2	28,584	14.29
Kenya	55,000	1	3,281	5.97
Korea	7,119,252	3	54,723	.77
Kuwait	400,000	2	509,957	127.49
Lebanon	600,000	3	73,573	12.26
Liberia	25,000	1	1,808	7.23

Figure 1. (*Continued*)

Name of Country	TV Sets in Use*	Networks or Equiv.*	Exported VCRs**	VCRs as % of TV Sets†
Libyan Arab Republic	235,000	1	188,734	80.31
Luxembourg	89,700	3	158	.18
Madagascar	8,200	1	410	5.00
Malaysia	1,051,272	4	233,334	22.20
Maldives	1,000	1	1,065	106.50
Mali	n/a	n/a	40	.00
Malta	89,057	1	139	.16
Mauritius	87,000	1	2,300	2.64
Mexico	8,500,000	1	44,694	.53
Monaco	17,000	1	n/a	.00
Mongolia	2,000	1	n/a	.00
Morocco	687,700	1	1,052	.15
Mozambique	3,500	1	179	5.11
Netherlands	6,189,000	2	887,348	14.34
Netherlands Antilles	50,000	3	5,862	11.72
New Caledonia	n/a	1	9,195	.00
New Zealand	922,182	2	99,227	10.76
Nicaragua	170,000	2	19	.01
Niger	9,800	1	270	2.76
Nigeria	500,000	1	20,035	4.01
Northern Mariana Islands	3,800	1	n/a	.00
Norway	1,540,447	1	283,464	18.40
Oman	40,000	1	49,995	124.99
Pakistan	873,657	1	2,517	.29
Panama	220,000	4	387,809	176.28
Paraguay	350,000	3	2,344	.67
Peoples Dem. Rep. of Yeman	30,000	1	n/a	.00
Peru	1,364,933	3	3,889	.28
Philippines	2,698,700	7	55,531	2.06
Poland	7,850,000	2	836	.01
Portugal	1,500,000	2	4,932	.33
Puerto Rico	n/a	n/a	19,027	.00
Qatar	100,000	2	68,443	68.44
Romania	3,897,000	2	299	.01
Samoa	4,500	5	71	1.58
Saudi Arabia	1,550,000	6	786,260	50.73
Senegal	1,700	1	350	20.59
Sierra Leone	8,000	2	304	3.80
Singapore	452,558	2	1,286,720	284.32
South Africa	2,000,000	3	486,804	24.34
Spain	9,573,000	2	779,150	8.14
Sri Lanka	90,000	2	12,242	13.60
Sudan	90,000	2	180	.20
Surinam	40,000	1	473	1.18
Swaziland	5,500	1	n/a	.00

continued

Figure 1. (*Continued*)

Name of Country	TV Sets in Use*	Networks or Equiv.*	Exported VCRs**	VCRs as % of TV Sets†
Sweden	3,235,255	2	468,513	14.48
Switzerland	2,072,181	3	507,156	24.47
Syria	700,000	1	17,886	2.56
Tanzania	7,152	1	56	.78
Thailand	720,000	8	97,287	13.51
Togo	10,500	2	n/a	.00
Trinidad & Tobago	235,000	1	n/a	.00
Tunisia	385,000	1	n/a	.00
Turkey	3,650,000	1	40,012	1.10
Uganda	65,000	1	n/a	.00
United Arab Emirates	100,000	2	505,162	505.16
United Kingdom	26,300,000	3	6,234,344	23.70
Upper Volta	7,700	1	647	8.40
Uruguay	350,000	10	1,324	.38
USA	180,800,000	3	12,998,828	7.19
USSR	70,000,000	4	5,357	.01
Venezuela	1,710,000	4	190,442	11.14
Vietnam	500,000	1	143	.03
West Germany	24,500,000	3	5,376,981	21.95
Yeman Arab Republic	n/a	1	4,289	.00
Yugoslavia	3,937,858	8	269	.01
Zaire	7,500	2	13,365	178.20
Zambia	260,000	1	226	.09
Zimbabwe	95,000	2	n/a	.00
Total:	560,426,688	296	39,922,363	7.12

*Television Digest Inc., *Television & Cable Factbook,* 1984. The estimated number of networks or network equivalents available to the typical television household is based on a reading of descriptive material in the *Factbook.*

**Japan Tariff Association, *Japan Exports & imports,* 1976-1983 editions.

†The data for Japan are misleading, since Japan does not import VCRs from itself. While only 30,403,046 TV sets are licensed by NHK, the Association of Electronic Equipment Industry says that there are about 50 million TV sets in Japan, or an average of 1.5 per household. Tokyo Broadcasting System says there are five Japanese networks: NHK, TBS, NTV, CX and ANB, although some have mixed or cross services.

Source: CBS Inc. Reprinted with permission.

Figure 2. Videocassette Recorders: National Figures

	Total (thousands) 1982	Percentage of TV homes 1982	Total (thousands) 1983 (est.)	Percentage of TV homes 1982 (est.)
Argentina	45	0.9	65	1.2
Australia	605	10.9	1,125	20.3
Austria	90	3.7	125	5.1
Bahrain	38	34.6	48	43.6
Belgium	190	6.1	240	7.7
Brazil	250	1.5	700	4.2
Canada	500	4.4	950	8.4
Chile	35	2.9	50	4.1
China	1	0.02	2	0.04
Colombia	175	7.4	275	11.6
Denmark	165	7.0	245	10.4
Ecuador	18	4.3	30	7.2
Egypt	30	0.6	100	2.0
Ethiopia	0.3	0.7	0.4	0.8
Finland	50	2.7	100	5.4
France	1,000	5.9	1,650	9.7
Germany, FR	2,650	12.6	3,900	18.5
Greece	25	1.5	40	2.4
Guyana	12	2.5	16	3.4
Hong Kong	185	15.2	300	24.0
India	180	11.6	530	34.2
Indonesia	200	12.5	250	15.6
Iran	240	11.4	285	13.5
Iraq	70	10.0	100	14.3
Ireland	150	18.0	200	23.0
Israel	25	6.25	40	10.0
Italy	175	1.2	250	1.7
Jamaica	6	3.6	13	7.8
Japan	3,420	11.8	7,560	26.1
Jordan	25	8.3	34	11.3
Kuwait	433	80.0	500	92.0
Lebanon	40	5.0	50	6.3
Malaysia	220	20.0	300	27.3
Mexico	90	1.2	125	1.7
Netherlands	420	9.9	605	14.1
New Zealand	25	2.9	40	4.6
Nigeria	7	0.7	13	1.3
Norway	158	13.0	250	20.5
Oman	25	50.0	35	70.0
Pakistan	250	16.7	350	23.4
Panama	150	68.2	180	81.8
Peru	100	11.4	150	17.1
Philippines	275	22.9	330	27.4
Poland	2	0.03	3	0.05

continued

Figure 2. (*Continued*)

	Total (thousands) 1982	Percentage of TV homes 1982	Total (thousands) 1983 (est.)	Percentage of TV homes 1982 (est.)
Portugal	65	4.5	86	6.0
Puerto Rico	100	11.0	120	13.2
Qatar	47	58.8	60	75.0
Saudi Arabia	450	14.5	600	19.3
Singapore	225	52.3	270	62.7
South Africa	120	5.5	160	7.3
Spain	280	2.9	450	4.7
Sri Lanka	10	14.7	15	22.1
Sweden	500	13.9	610	17.0
Switzerland	215	8.0	298	11.1
Syria	15	3.8	20	5.1
Taiwan	525	14.6	725	20.2
Tanzania	1	13.9	1	13.9
Thailand	30	3.6	45	5.4
United Arab Emirates	65	65.0	75	75.0
United Kingdom	3,625	19.0	5,750	30.1
USA	5,250	6.4	8.750	10.7
USSR	1	0.001	2	0.003
Venezuela	220	12.6	400	22.9

Source: Adapted with permission from *InterMedia,* July/September 1983, p. 39. Compiled by David Fisher. © 1983 International Institute of Communications.

Figure 3. VCR Penetration, End of 1984

Region	Country	VCRs (thousands)
Europe	U.K.	6,700
	West Germany	4,900
	France	2,200
	Spain	1,100
	Netherlands	950
	Sweden	715
	Switzerland	350
	Belgium	325
	Austria	275
	Norway	270
Asia	Japan	13,900
	Taiwan	850
	India	610
	Indonesia	600
	Malaysia	450
	Thailand	400
	Singapore	400

Figure 3. (*Continued*)

Region	Country	VCRs (thousands)
	Pakistan	200
	China	75
North America	United States	16,400
	Canada	1,600
	Bermuda	22
Middle East	Turkey	2,200
	Saudi Arabia	840
	Kuwait	400
	Israel	350
	Lebanon	300
	Iran	200
South America	Venezuela	500
	Colombia	400
	Brazil	380
	Argentina	60
Oceania	Australia	1,960
	New Zealand	180
	Fiji Islands	15
Africa	South Africaa	485
	Egypt	190
	Kenya	140
Central America	Mexico	400
	Panama	50
	Honduras	8
	El Salvador	6
	Costa Rica	5
Caribbean	Puerto Rico	120
	Trinidad and Tobago	115

(The world's VCR population was 42,172,000 in 1983; 66,244,000 in 1984; and in 1985 will "top 100,000,000", according to the Motion Picture Export Association of America.

Source: Excerpted from " '85 VCR Count to Tally 100-Mil, Predicts MPEA," *Variety,* February 27, 1985, p. 37. Figures collected by the Motion Picture Export Association of America. Data from the Electronics Industries Assn. and other trade groups worldwide. Reprinted with permission.

Author Index

Subject Index